The History & Mystery
of Dinosaurs and Man

# Chronicles
## of
# Dinosauria

Master
Books®
A Division of New Leaf Publishing Group
www.masterbooks.net

"Dave Woetzel brings not only a biblical understanding of dinosaurs to the table, he offers his exciting personal experiences and research as well. He has been on a life adventure in which we all can share and from which we all can benefit. All Christian families and leaders can learn much from this readable book!"

— John Morris, President, Institute for Creation Research

"If you're looking for an authoritative discussion with beautiful graphics on dinosaurs, the new book by David Woetzel and Richard Dobbs Jr. entitled *Chronicles of Dinosauria* is a great addition to your library. It's accurate, beautiful, and biblical."

— Larry Vardiman, Retired Biblical Paleontologist, Institute for Creation Research

"People everywhere — not just children! — seem to be fascinated by the origin, nature, and destiny of dinosaurs. The Bible speaks clearly of their co-existence with mankind. David Woetzel explains this, and has also done a remarkable job of collecting supporting evidence from fossils, history, and art."

— Dr. John Whitcomb, Co-author of the landmark creation book *The Genesis Flood*

"Dinosaurs are used more than any other animal to promote evolutionary type thinking. It is so refreshing to see a book on this subject that honors God. Dave Woetzel has put together an excellent book on this subject."

— Buddy Davis, Adventurer and Paleo-artist Answers in Genesis

"I highly recommend this treasure-trove of evidence and information about dinosaurs and how they have interacted with people, from the beginning of creation, through the Genesis Flood and the Ice Age, and even possibly today."

— D. Russell Humphreys, Physicist, Board Member, Creation Research Society

# Chronicles
## of
# Dinosauria

written by
**Dave Woetzel**

illustrated by
**Richard Dobbs Jr.**

First Printing: April 2013

Master Books®, P.O. Box 726, Green Forest, AR 72638

Master Books® is a division of the New Leaf Publishing Group, Inc.

ISBN: 978-0-89051-704-8

Library of Congress Number: 2012956094

Please consider requesting that a copy of this volume be purchased by your local library system.

All Scripture is from the King James Version of the Bible

## Printed in China

Please visit our website for other great titles: www.masterbooks.net

For information regarding author interviews,
please contact the publicity department at (870) 438-5288

Quetzelcoatlus

## Author's Acknowledgments

Special thanks to the following reviewers: Vance Nelson, Ian Juby, Kurt Woetzel, Ruth Davis, Annie Southard, and Dr. John Whitcomb. I am indebted to my supportive wife, Gloria, who encourages my cryptozoology effort and my numerous expeditions. The credit for initiating this book goes to the illustrator, Richard Dobbs.

Woetzel in
Amazon dugout

## Author's Introduction

Why is it important that we carefully study the past to achieve a proper view of origins? It is critical because such study sets up our worldview and becomes foundational to our whole philosophy of life today. Are we accountable to a Creator, or merely a cosmic biological accident?

The Bible states: "For the invisible things of him from the creation of the world are clearly seen, being understood by the things that are made, even his eternal power and Godhead" (Romans 1:20). A marvelous creation should inform us about the Designer and Maker of all that we observe around us, from the majestic mountains to the expansive oceans; from the starry cosmic light show to the incredible complexity of the single-celled bacteria.

As we dig into the earth and seek to understand biological origins, we are inescapably drawn to the great reptiles . . . the pterosaurs, plesiosaurs, and dinosaurs! People of all ages are naturally fascinated and awed by these fearsome creatures.

A dragon depiction outside the Church of St. Louis
of the French, built in Rome during the 1500s

Indeed, the Bible indicates that God approves of our contemplation of the mighty beasts He created. In Job 40:15, God commanded his servant to such consideration: "Behold now behemoth. . . ." Shortly thereafter the Lord explained His reason for commending this. Job 41:10 states: "None is so fierce that dare stir him up: who then is able to stand before me?" The mighty dinosaurs should draw our attention to the Almighty Creator to whom we will all give account.

But evolutionists have co-opted the public attraction toward the great reptiles to sell their theories of origins. A leading Darwinist wrote, "Dinosaurs . . . are the poster children of evolution, and they inspire the vast majority of those who touch them."[1]

As a young man I was distressed with such evolutionary propaganda when I attended a local museum of science. Always the dinosaurs are portrayed as having died out millions of years before man evolved. Evolutionists are unequivocal that "No human being has ever seen a live dinosaur."[2] One of the goals of my life became to reclaim the terrible lizards to the glory of our incredible Creator. I began to assemble the evidence that men and dinosaurs co-existed and eventually presented it at the Genesis Park website. The tagline for the web page is "Dinosaurs: living evidence of a powerful Creator." This book lays out the evidence that dinosaurs and man coexisted for the reader's consideration:

- the biblical evidence
- the historical evidence
- the artistic evidence
- the fossil evidence
- and the cryptozoology evidence.

Cryptozoology involves researching reports of animals that have yet to be proven to exist, like the Loch Ness Monster. Some of these animals have been recorded in myths and legends but have not yet been positively identified by scientists. Others are known from the fossil record but are thought to be extinct. A great example of a cryptozoology success involves the fish

Caddy surveillance in Puget Sound

Poling in the Bangweulu of Zambia

known as the coelacanth. Evolutionary paleontologists believed it to be extinct since the Cretaceous period (the time of the dinosaurs) almost 65 million years ago. Then one was discovered in 1938 off the shores of South Africa and a second species was found in 1999 in Indonesia. The fish lives in waters a few hundred feet or more below the surface. Now referred to as a living fossil, the coelacanth reminds us that there could be many more surprising discoveries yet to be made!

I believe that I am in a unique position to discuss the cryptozoology evidence, having personally visited each of the locations that are highlighted here, some of them multiple times. A number of other potential cryptid locations that I researched have not been included. The standard I have used for inclusion involves multiple independent lines of evidence. For example, ancient Native American legends, modern-day sightings, and artwork on rock all provide evidence for the existence of Ogopogo. Perhaps one day soon God will allow us to capture one of these magnificent creatures, forcing even the most ardent skeptic of the Genesis account to concede that man has coexisted with dinosaurs, just as the Bible has said all along.

TITANOCERATOPS
74.5 MILLION YEARS OLD

Museums showcase the evolutionary speculation about dinosaurs.

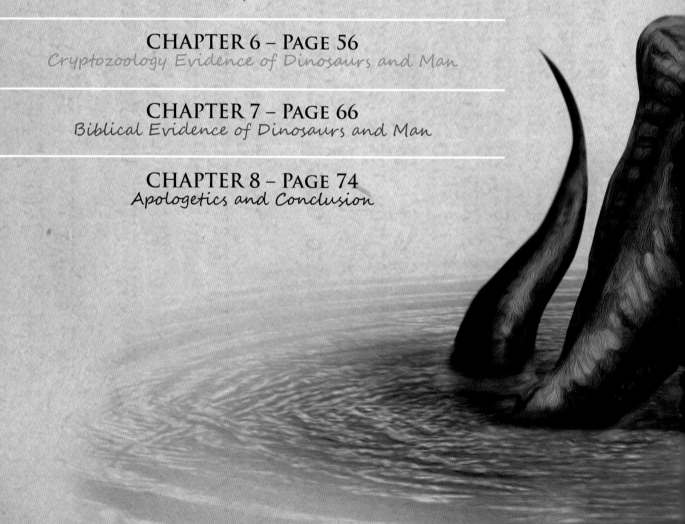

Concavenator

### GENESIS CHAPTER 1

29 And God said, Behold, I have given you every herb bearing seed, which is upon the face of all the earth, and every tree, in the which is the fruit of a tree yielding seed; to you it shall be for meat.

30 And to every beast of the earth, and to every fowl of the air, and to every thing that creepeth upon the earth, wherein there is life, I have given every green herb for meat: and it was so.

# CHAPTER 1
## The Creation and the Dinosaurs

Therizinosaurs

Although we cannot travel back in time to see the first dinosaurs, we do have an eyewitness report from the only person who was on hand to observe their origin, God Himself. On the fifth day of creation, "God created great whales [literally sea monsters in the original Hebrew], and every living creature that moveth, which the waters brought forth abundantly, after their kind, and every winged fowl after his kind: and God saw that it was good" (Genesis 1:21). These "sea monsters" would include plesiosaurs, the great swimming reptiles. The flying creatures would have been created on the same day, including the great reptilian pterosaurs that once filled the skies of the early earth.

# THE FIRST DINOSAURS

"And God made the beast of the earth after his kind, and cattle after their kind, and every thing that creepeth upon the earth after his kind: and God saw that it was good"
(Genesis 1:25).

Amargasaurus

## Animal Kinds vs. Species

Although the great flying and swimming reptiles are usually presented alongside the dinosaurs, they are classified differently by scientists. Dinosaurs are reptiles that walked on land and the Bible describes their creation just a few verses later, lumping them in among the "creeping things" and "beasts of the earth." As God spoke, each of the dinosaurian kinds sprang into existence, coming up out of the ground. Wouldn't it have been an amazing sight to see a large dinosaur like a T. rex coming up? Along with the dinosaurs that God created on the sixth day, He also made man out of the dust of the ground.

Built into the original dinosaur kinds that God created was the capacity for a great deal of genetic variation. This would have been exhibited in subsequent generations of great reptiles, just like we have hundreds of dog breeds that have developed from an original wild dog kind (likely gray wolves).

A biblical "kind" is much broader than a species and would include all varieties of a particular family of plants or animals that could interbreed. For example, it is quite likely that all of the large sauropod species (like Diplodocus, Apatosaurus, Brachiosaurus, etc.) were varieties of a single created kind.

The ideal conditions on the early earth would have allowed for rapid multiplication and diversification of reptile kinds. By studying large nesting sites, like those discovered in central India, scientists have learned that dinosaurs could lay a dozen or more eggs in a single nest. If they were like modern lizards, they might lay several clutches of eggs in a single breeding season.

These original dinosaurians would not have been like the terrifying monsters portrayed in Hollywood movies. The Bible tells us that "God saw every thing that he had made, and, behold, it was very good" (Genesis 1:31). The first dinosaurs would have consumed only plants as they peacefully lived alongside Adam and Eve on the early earth (Genesis 1:29–30). It was not until mankind sinned, disobeying God and heeding the wicked serpent Satan, that God brought a Curse upon all creation.

Pain, suffering, carnivorous activity, and ultimately death, all followed from God's just judgment upon sin. "Wherefore, as by one man sin entered into the world, and death by sin; and so death passed upon all men, for that all have sinned" (Romans 5:12).

Allosaurs attacking a Camarasaurus

13

Dilophosaurus

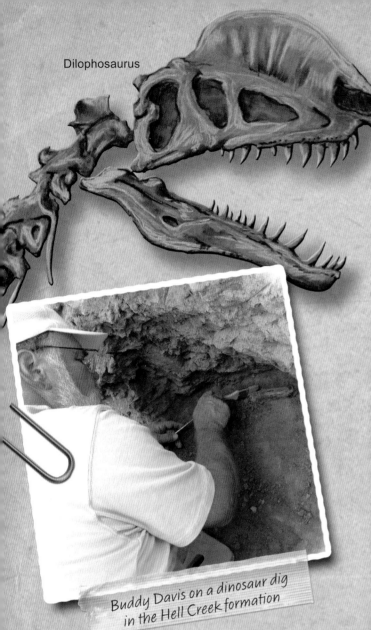

Buddy Davis on a dinosaur dig
in the Hell Creek formation

## Studying Dinosaur Fossils

We can learn much about dinosaurs by studying their fossils (preserved bones, footprints, droppings, eggs, etc.). By piecing together the evidence like a detective, paleontologists can accurately reassemble the skeletons of these awe-inspiring creatures and give us a glimpse into how they lived thousands of years ago, filling in details not given to us in God's revealed Word.

There are still many things that we don't know about the dinosaurs — puzzles awaiting further scientific discoveries. For example, the debate still rages about whether dinosaurs were cold-blooded or warm-blooded. And we are not quite sure how the mighty pterosaurs, like the Quetzalcoatlus with a wingspan of 50 feet, could stay aloft.

Some scientific theories and speculations directly contradict God's Word and cannot be true. For example, evolutionists tell stories about dinosaurs existing millions of years before man "evolved." Further, they invent theories regarding certain dinosaurs evolving into birds.

Evolutionists have not, however, come to any agreement on where dinosaurs came from. The great reptiles appear abruptly in the fossil record, just as if they were suddenly created. Of course, this agrees perfectly with what the Bible states in Genesis.

## DINOSAURS WORLDWIDE

Thousands of dinosaur species have been discovered around the world, from Alaska to the Antarctic. Different types of dinosaurs ranged in weight from four pounds, in the case of little Compsognathus, up to 160,000 pounds, in the case of the great sauropods like Brachiosaurus.

# THE EARLY EARTH

Dinosaurians were not the only creatures to grow large on the early earth. The Bible records that there were giant men in those days as well (Genesis 6:4). In fact, one of the secrets of the fossil record is that virtually all animal kinds were bigger, and arguably healthier in the distant past. Preserved remains found in what is now the desert

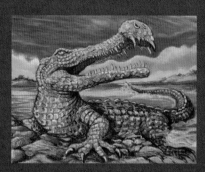

of Niger tell of a hyper-crocodile that would have feasted on dinosaurs in what was then a verdant river valley. Fossil ferns the size of modern trees have been discovered and horsetails once shot up over thirty feet tall. There were big cockroaches, as well as crickets, grasshoppers, and monstrous spiders that thrived in a place of endless summer. Dragonflies with a three-foot wingspan skimmed over swamps in which eight-foot beavers and sixty-foot cattails flourished. Beetles once grew to be the size of a baseball mitt and climbed up conifers that towered a hundred feet high. Skeletons have been found of sixty-foot long sharks. A giant guinea pig grew as big as a modern rhinoceros while the ancient rhino grew as big as a two-story building.

Plants and animals are not evolving from simple to complex. Rather they are degenerating from the original created condition due to factors like genetic mutations and environmental degradation. Scientific advances in nutrition and medicine temporarily increased human health and lifespan, but ultimately our world is running down (Romans 8:22) and has been deteriorating from God's good creation.

There is evidence that environmental conditions were quite different on the early earth. Tropical vegetation and animals that thrive in warm climates have been found frozen in Antarctica. Explorations of the Siberian Arctic have yielded an abundance of fossils (mammoth, woolly rhinos, musk ox, antelope, deer, bear, horse, and many more), requiring forests and meadows to sustain them. Embedded in Arctic muck are a large number of mammals that have been frozen before they could decay.

God had commanded His creation in Genesis 1 to "be fruitful and multiply." In Chapter 6 of Genesis, the Bible describes how men began to multiply upon the earth.

We know from the many fossil sites that dinosaurs also multiplied greatly, filling whole regions of the earth. There is evidence that the early earth was divided into distinct geographical living areas (called biomes) with fully functioning communities of plants and animals unique to each. The great reptiles dominated vast inland lake and swamp regions. Tropical plants and reptiles are today found frozen at the poles, showing that the whole earth was once much warmer. In Alaska, various duck-billed dinosaurs, turtles, conifers, herbaceous vegetation, and broad-leaved trees bear testimony to a temperate environment that once existed there. This made for optimal reptile habitat and resulted in a golden era for dinosaurs.

Herds of plant-eating dinosaurs roamed, like cows, across the marshy grasslands. The gigantic herbivorous sauropods could retreat to the safety of the waters, leaving only their long necks sticking out. Meat-eating dinosaurs like the carnivorous Allosaurus and Velociraptor would have roved the shoreline, picking off the young and the sick, scavenging carrion, and digging up eggs for food. Some dinosaurs, like the armored Ankylosaurus, protected themselves with spikes and club-like tails. The horned ceratopsians carried spears on their heads for self-defense, much like a buffalo or rhinoceros.

It is likely that the human population (and many other mammals) would have occupied a separate biome at a higher elevation, well above the swamplands. There they established the first civilization, building cities and pursuing scientific endeavors like metallurgy (processing bronze and iron). However, as the growing human population began to enjoy leisure, feasting, and music, man's corruption also grew. "And God saw that the wickedness of man was great in the earth, and that every imagination of the thoughts of his heart was only evil continually. And it repented the Lord that he had made man on the earth, and it grieved him at his heart. And the Lord said, I will destroy man whom I have created from the face of the earth; both man, and beast, and the creeping thing, and the fowls of the air; for it repenteth me that I have made them." (Genesis 6:5-7) God determined to send a worldwide flood to destroy that entire civilization.

**DINO TRIVIA:** Did you know that the name dinosaur is Greek for "terrible lizard"? It was coined by the British anatomist Richard Owen in 1842. (Before that the great reptiles were called dragons.) Interestingly, Owen's expressed purpose for creating the new taxonomical order, Dinosauria, was to debunk evolutionary ideas. Since these monstrous creatures had become extinct long ago, Owen argued, the gradual progression from primitive to advanced species claimed by evolutionists must be false.[3]

## CHAPTER 2

The Flood and
the Dinosaurs

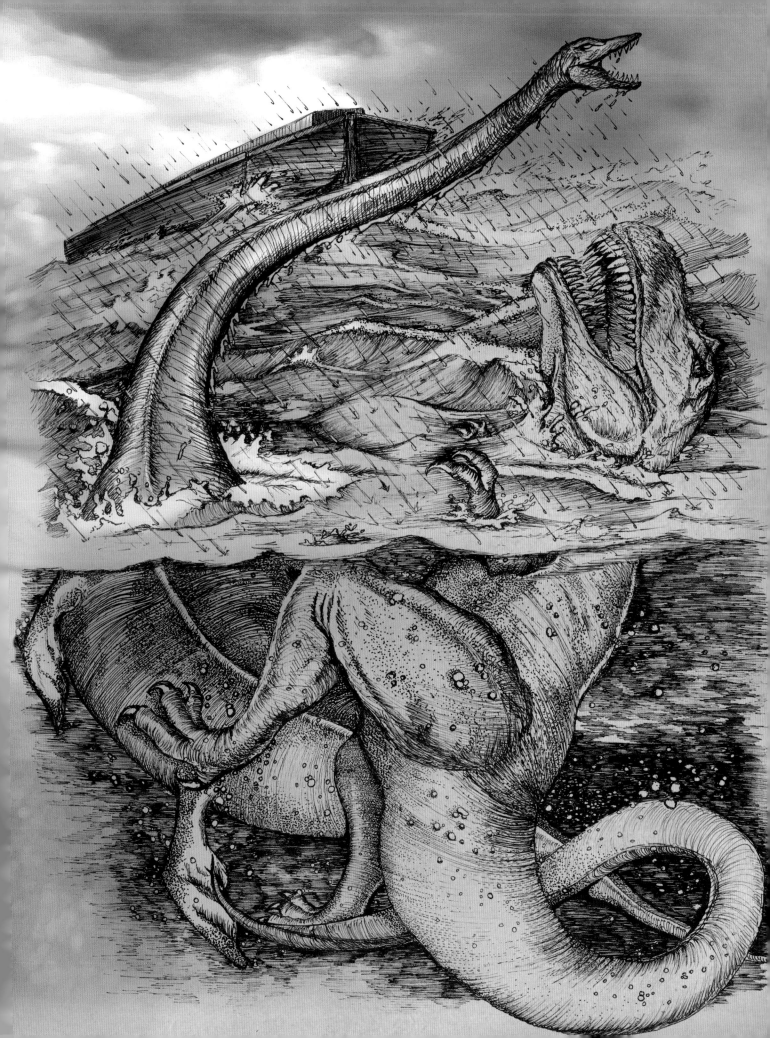

Dimetrodon

In the midst of the wicked pre-Flood civilization, there remained a righteous man, Noah, who followed God with his family. God instructed Noah to build a massive ark, large enough to carry two of each kind of land animal. This would have included each of the original created dinosaur and pterosaur kinds.

It is quite likely that smaller juveniles would have been taken aboard to represent the larger dinosaur and pterosaur families. The plesiosaurs would not need to be on board since they could freely roam the entire globe during the Flood.

Apparently it took a century of work to build the huge boat, prepare provisions, and load up all the animals that God would bring to Noah (Genesis 6:3). The God-given dimensions of the ark were

vast. Picture a three-story barge that is longer than a football field!

Finally, all the preparations by Noah, his wife, his three sons, and their wives were completed. The Bible makes the point that once they were all aboard in the place of refuge, the Lord Himself shut the door (Genesis 7:16). Not only did this ensure a tight seal against the storm to come, but it vividly pictures God closing the door on that entire generation that had rejected Him.

As the Flood began, the people in the surrounding area would undoubtedly have had a change of heart and come knocking at the ark. Even if Noah's compassion had swayed him to allow them aboard, God had fixed the door tightly.

18

# The Onslaught Of The Flood

The Bible details the onslaught of the Genesis Flood: "In the six hundredth year of Noah's life, in the second month, the seventeenth day of the month, the same day were all the fountains of the great deep broken up, and the windows of heaven were opened. And the rain was upon the earth forty days and forty nights" (Genesis 7:11–12). The initiating event of the great Flood was tectonic earth movements, releasing water high into the atmosphere and shifting the continental plates. This contributed most of the Flood water that gradually rose to destroy the early earth.

The Bible is very clear that the Flood covered the entire earth with sufficient depth that the highest mountain would clear the draft of the ark: "Fifteen cubits upward did the waters prevail; and the mountains were covered. And all flesh died that moved upon the earth, both of fowl, and of cattle, and of beast, and of every creeping thing that creepeth upon the earth, and every man: All in whose nostrils was the breath of life, of all that was in the dry land, died" (Genesis 7:20-22).

The earthquake and volcanic activity would have initiated tsunamis, and the marine life was the first to be buried by submarine landslides. Fast-moving currents carrying debris deposited multiple layers simultaneously, forming sediments that would later harden into rocks.

The earth's lower biomes were covered first, including the dinosaurs in the swamps. Later, the mammals were carried downstream amidst the tremendous erosion and mudflows from the 40 days of rain. Fossil graveyards formed as creatures that struggled to get to higher elevations were overwhelmed, swept up in the waves and currents, and then covered in mass graveyards. The last creatures to die were the most mobile, including the birds.

## GLOBAL FLOOD

Did you know that there is a universal Flood belief in the traditions and language of every major nationality, including Babylonians, Chinese, Native Americans, Indians, Greeks, Norse, Sumerians, Egyptians, Hawaiians, and many more (over 270 in all)? Various details match up with the original biblical account, like the Flood waters coming from the ground covering the whole earth, the name Noah, the number of family members, the huge ark, and all the land animals aboard.

Coelophysis fossils found in a
mass gravesite at Ghost Ranch
Quarry in New Mexico

Fossil Graveyard

# The Prevailing of the Flood

The waters continued to cover the globe for 150 days. Animals trapped in sediments died and their remains began to experience various fossilizing processes. The preservation process called permineralization involves minerals filling in the cell tissue and crystallizing to preserve the original form and some of the original organic material.

Fossilization occurs quickly when great pressure is exerted and the right minerals are present. The fossil fuels, like coal and oil, that we use to power our modern civilization would have been formed largely during this portion of the Flood.

Today we see the evidence of the Flood in large-scale rock layers covering vast geographic areas, like the Morrison Formation that covers much of western North America and coal seams that cover over 100,000 square miles. Scientists find the remains of sea creatures on the tops of mountains all over the earth.

Relics of the great Flood that buried the dinosaurs include huge boulders that were transported hundreds of miles by moving currents and tall erosional remnants like Devil's Tower in Wyoming and Ship Rock in New Mexico that remained after the retreating Flood waters carved the landscape.

Many of our best dinosaur fossils come from the vast fossil graveyards of animal remains that are found throughout the world. These formations are difficult for the evolutionists to explain via processes observed today. Ongoing excavations in the Gobi Desert

Ship Rock in New Mexico

revealed 25 theropod dinosaurs along with 200 skulls of mammals.[4] The desolate Gobi is not unique.

In the United States, one finds a profusion of skeletons in a hillside dinosaur graveyard in New Mexico and in the famous Bone Cabin Quarry of Wyoming. In Alberta, Canada, there is a huge burial site that stretches for hundreds of miles and holds innumerable dinosaur bones. In Agate Springs, Nebraska, a fossil graveyard contains 9,000 animals that were found buried in alluvial deposits (from flowing water). The remains of hundreds of rhinos, three-toed horses, camels, giant wild boars, birds, plants, trees, seashells, and fish are mixed and intermingled in great confusion. In Tanzania, Belgium, Mongolia, and elsewhere, massive numbers of creatures lie trapped in sediments and debris best explained by a large-scale flood. Some have speculated that "The Karoo formation in South Africa alone contains fossil remains of about 800 billion animals."[5]

## AMBER

Fossilized tree pitch or resin is called amber. Some amber contains insects or air bubbles that have been preserved and give us insight into the primeval world. Analysis suggests that the early earth atmosphere was denser and contained more oxygen, conditions that may have led to longer, healthier life for both men and dinosaurs.

# The Abatement of the Flood

Over the course of another 150 days, God mercifully brought the Flood to an end. The ocean basins sank down; the continental plates rose up (Psalm 104); and the waters ran off into the sea. The sheet-like flowing of the receding waters carved out notches in the mountains, eroded the freshly laid sediments, formed vast canyons, and deposited material into the oceans to form the continental shelf. Fossilized dinosaur bones were left exposed for subsequent generations to excavate.

In Genesis 8 we read, "And God spake unto Noah, saying, Go forth of the ark, thou, and thy wife, and thy sons, and thy sons' wives with thee. Bring forth with thee every living thing that is with thee, of all flesh, both of fowl, and of cattle, and of every creeping thing that creepeth upon the earth; that they may breed abundantly in the earth, and be fruitful, and multiply upon the earth" (15–17). As the dinosaurs and other animals came off the ark, God repeated His command to fill the lands.

Earth's creatures would have rapidly diversified within their kinds and migrated to occupy the empty habitats around the world. Abundant floating brush and tree debris from the Flood would have served as rafts to carry animals to distant land masses.

## The Ice Age

But the climate would have been dramatically different after the Flood. Volcanic dust and changed atmospheric conditions led to cooling over the continents, while warm oceans generated a lot of rain and snow. This brought on an Ice Age that prevailed for centuries after the great Flood. Great volumes of water were stored up in the glaciers, especially at the poles, creating land bridges between the continents. However, the harsher winters were better suited to the warm-blooded mammals and birds, resulting in many kinds of dinosaurs becoming extinct. While some dinosaur species survived in tropical regions and others adapted somewhat to the seasons, the golden age of the great reptiles was over.

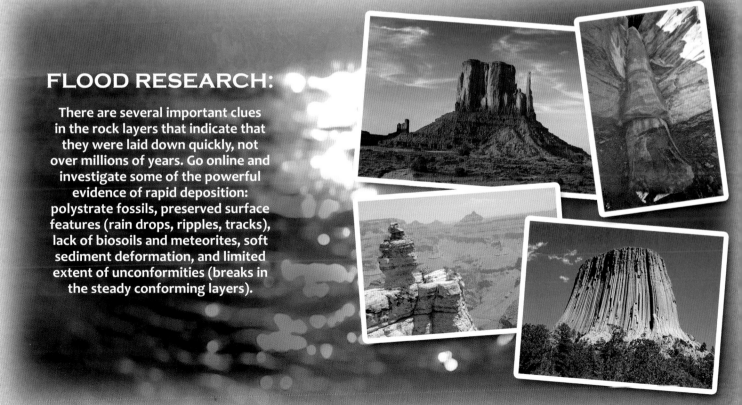

## FLOOD RESEARCH:

There are several important clues in the rock layers that indicate that they were laid down quickly, not over millions of years. Go online and investigate some of the powerful evidence of rapid deposition: polystrate fossils, preserved surface features (rain drops, ripples, tracks), lack of biosoils and meteorites, soft sediment deformation, and limited extent of unconformities (breaks in the steady conforming layers).

# CHAPTER 3

## Fossil Evidence
## of Dinosaurs
## and Man

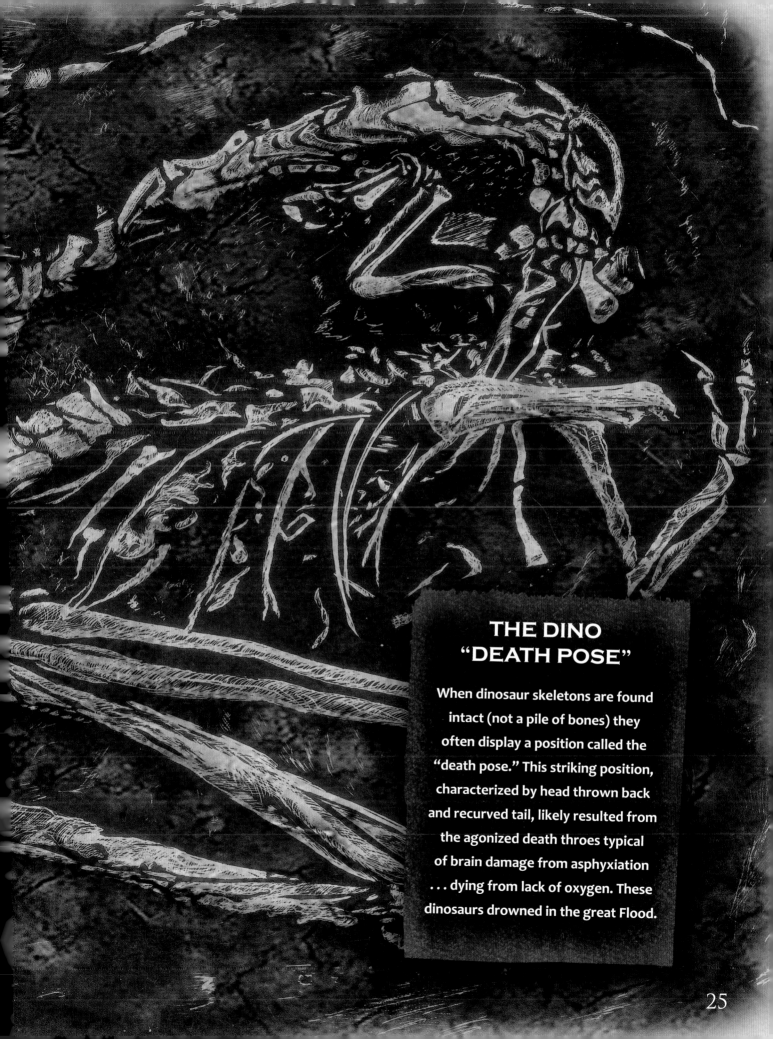

## THE DINO "DEATH POSE"

When dinosaur skeletons are found intact (not a pile of bones) they often display a position called the "death pose." This striking position, characterized by head thrown back and recurved tail, likely resulted from the agonized death throes typical of brain damage from asphyxiation . . . dying from lack of oxygen. These dinosaurs drowned in the great Flood.

Tuatara

## Studying Bones

Today, thousands of years after the great catastrophe of Noah's day, scientists dig up the fossilized remains of the dinosaurs buried in the Genesis Flood. With only bones to analyze, scientists speculate and propose competing interpretations of what really happened to these dinosaurs.

Some evolutionists argue that they all died out 60 million years ago due to a giant asteroid that struck the earth and disrupted the climate. But if that were true, why did the crocodiles, thin-skinned lizards, and tuataras survive? If dinosaurs all disappeared off the earth long before man evolved from an ape-like ancestor, then no human being should ever have seen a live dinosaur. But there are several lines of evidence that dinosaurs and man did, in fact, co-exist. Some of the key indications come from the fossils themselves.

Kuehneosaurus and Icarosaurus resemble the flying dragon Draco, which is still found in southeastern Asia.

The fossil evidence can be grouped into two general categories: human artifacts and activities preserved in the lower layers of the fossil record, alongside or below dinosaur remnants; and clues that dinosaurs' bones themselves are not millions of years old. God clearly stated that the purpose of the Genesis Flood was to destroy the wicked pre-Flood civilization. So it is not surprising that we only find a few antediluvian human articles preserved.

# Human Artifacts in the Lower Fossil Record

In 1944, as a ten-year-old boy, Newton Anderson dropped and broke a lump of coal in his basement. He found that it contained a bell inside. The bituminous coal that was mined near his house in Upshur County, West Virginia, is thought by evolutionary geologists to have formed 300 million years ago. What was a bronze bell with an iron clapper doing in coal ascribed to the Carboniferous Period?

The Institute for Creation Research had the bell submitted to the lab at the University of Oklahoma. There, a nuclear activation analysis revealed that the bell's exact mix of metals was different from any known modern alloy production.

The bell was prominently featured in the 1992 CBS docudrama *Ancient Secrets of the Bible* and is now part of the Genesis Park collection. Newton spent a great deal of time researching the demon sculpted atop the bell. He discovered similarities to the Babylonian Southwest Wind Devil and the Hindu deity Garuda. Garuda is sometimes depicted on top of bells, as is the Egyptian Isis. Demonic worship seems to take on similar forms in various cultures. Mr. Anderson volunteered to take a lie-detector test to validate his claims. He was examined by an expert polygraph specialist and was found to be trustworthy.

Various other artifacts have been discovered in coal, including a cast iron pot found in a seam at the Municipal Electric Plant in Thomas, Oklahoma, that is now archived at Creation Evidence Museum. Another fascinating find in their museum collection is called the London Artifact. In June of 1934, members of the Hahn family discovered a rock with wood protruding from it. They chiseled it open, exposing the hammer head. The artifact was found near London, Texas, by a waterfall on Red Creek. This site is part of the Edwards Plateau and its rocks contain dinosaur remains. The wood handle is partially petrified and the head is made out of a rare iron mixture with chlorine. It would seem that the owner of this tool quite literally "missed the boat!"

Publications in the 19th century, before the evolutionary paradigm became widely accepted in archaeology, document artifacts discovered from a number of sites around the world showing human activity low in the geologic record.[6] These include flint tools that bear evidence of human workmanship, like the scraping and boring utensils found in the Red Crag Formation in England (dated to millions of years ago).

A small zinc and silver vessel was found in a Massachusetts rock layer supposed to be 600 million years old. Advanced stone tools were found in California gold mines. Professor J.D. Whitney, the state geologist of California, published a lengthy review of these implements, including spear points, mortars, and pestles, verifying that they were found deep in mine shafts underneath thick, undisturbed layers of lava thought to be from 9 to 55 million years old.

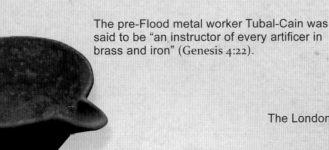

The pre-Flood metal worker Tubal-Cain was said to be "an instructor of every artificer in brass and iron" (Genesis 4:22).

The London Artifact.

Photo by David Lines

27

Photo by David Lines

Delk Trak

Acrocanthosaurus — A likely candidate responsible for tracks with humans at Glen Rose, Texas

## Footprints

The Paluxy River area of Glen Rose, Texas, is famous for its wonderfully preserved dinosaur tracks in stone. Human footprints in these same layers made headlines in the 1970s and 1980s when John Morris of the Institute for Creation Research wrote the popular book *Tracking Those Incredible Dinosaurs (and the People Who Knew Them)* and the film *Footprints in Stone* was produced by Stan Taylor. Over time, these original prints became quite worn and eroded. Evolutionists argued that they were merely elongated dinosaur footprints that had experienced infilling.[7]

The lack of clarity prompted most creationists to cease using the Paluxy footprints as evidence. But more recent discoveries have been much clearer and have given new force to the argument. After multiple trips to Glen Rose to personally examine the evidence and considerable dialogue with those opposed to the "man tracks," I came away convinced that the Sir George, Japanese, and feminine prints are authentic.

The Alvis Delk track came to light in 2008. What is particularly compelling about this artifact is that there is a human footprint intruded by a tridactyl dinosaur print. The Delk track has been subjected to extensive CAT scans to confirm authenticity. The compression

(greater density) underneath both prints can be observed in the matrix, indicating that the prints were formed while the material was soft, rather than carved after the fact. Though the controversy still rages, the Paluxy River research merits close watching.

A human footprint called the Zapata track was found in Permian limestone (thought to be 250–300 million years old) in New Mexico. It is a very shallow track, almost invisible unless wet and shown with strong side lighting. This accounts for the dramatic hour-glass shape with dots in front, similar to what you see when someone walks with wet feet on a cement floor. Geologist Don Patton attempted to cut this print out of the rock, but wore out four carborundum blades trying to make one cut!

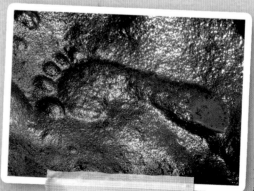

Photo by Don Patton

*Zapata track*

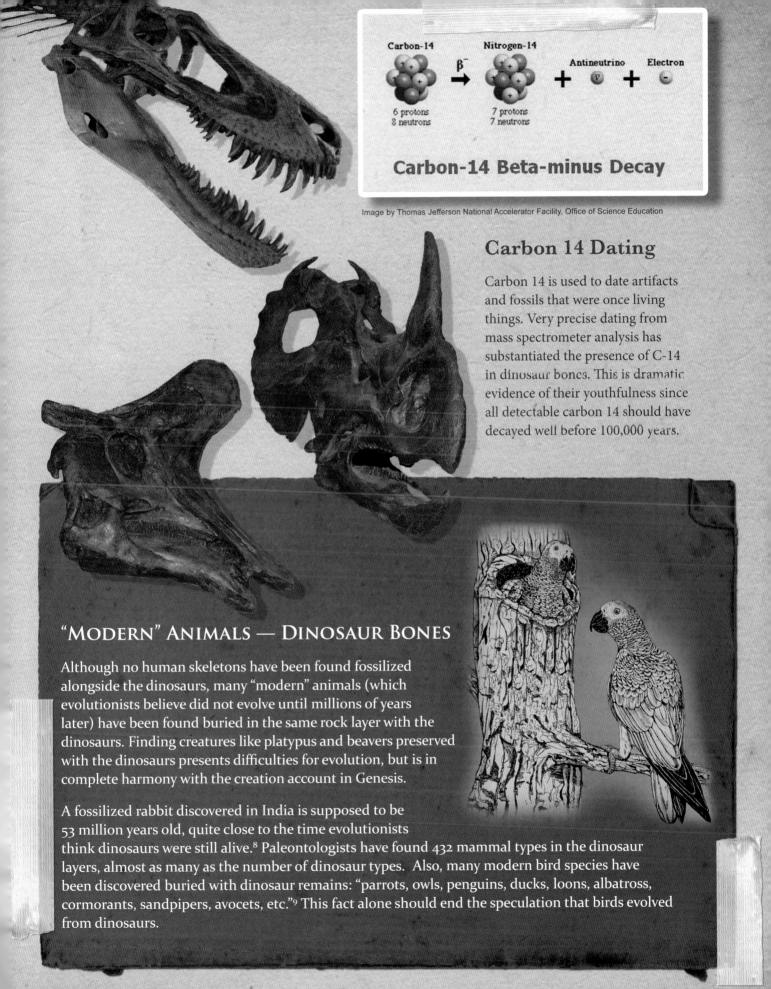

## Carbon-14 Beta-minus Decay

Carbon-14 → Nitrogen-14 + Antineutrino + Electron

6 protons
8 neutrons

7 protons
7 neutrons

Image by Thomas Jefferson National Accelerator Facility, Office of Science Education

## Carbon 14 Dating

Carbon 14 is used to date artifacts and fossils that were once living things. Very precise dating from mass spectrometer analysis has substantiated the presence of C-14 in dinosaur bones. This is dramatic evidence of their youthfulness since all detectable carbon 14 should have decayed well before 100,000 years.

## "Modern" Animals — Dinosaur Bones

Although no human skeletons have been found fossilized alongside the dinosaurs, many "modern" animals (which evolutionists believe did not evolve until millions of years later) have been found buried in the same rock layer with the dinosaurs. Finding creatures like platypus and beavers preserved with the dinosaurs presents difficulties for evolution, but is in complete harmony with the creation account in Genesis.

A fossilized rabbit discovered in India is supposed to be 53 million years old, quite close to the time evolutionists think dinosaurs were still alive.[8] Paleontologists have found 432 mammal types in the dinosaur layers, almost as many as the number of dinosaur types.  Also, many modern bird species have been discovered buried with dinosaur remains: "parrots, owls, penguins, ducks, loons, albatross, cormorants, sandpipers, avocets, etc."[9] This fact alone should end the speculation that birds evolved from dinosaurs.

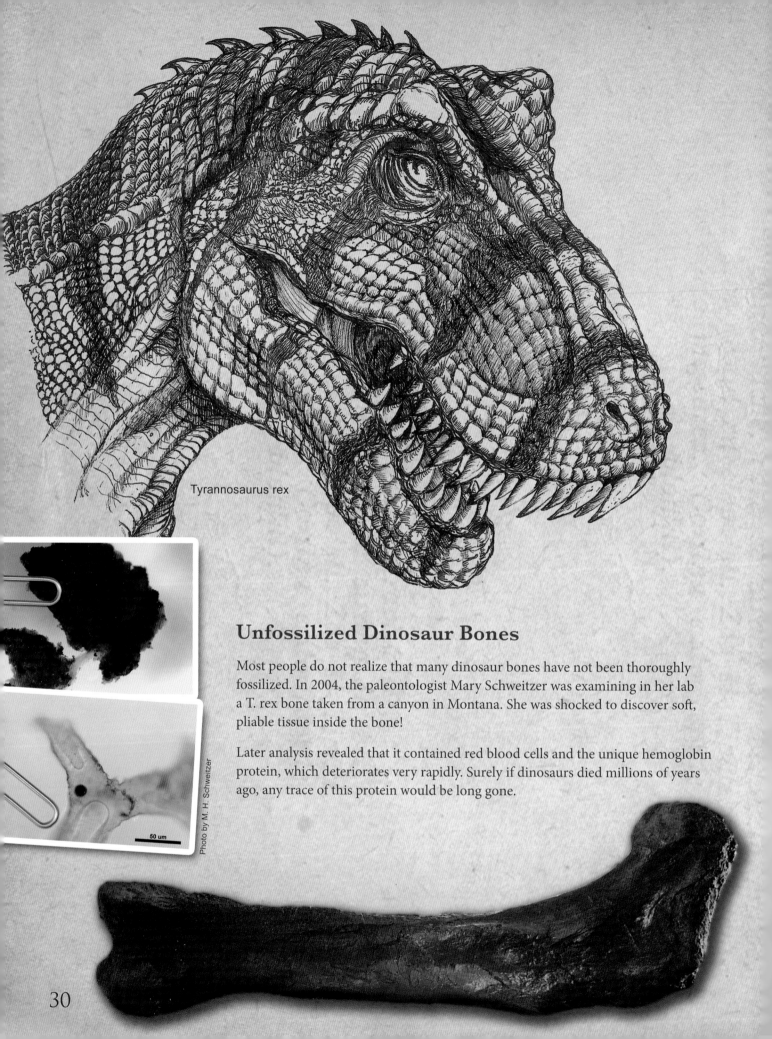

Tyrannosaurus rex

Photo by M. H. Schweitzer

## Unfossilized Dinosaur Bones

Most people do not realize that many dinosaur bones have not been thoroughly fossilized. In 2004, the paleontologist Mary Schweitzer was examining in her lab a T. rex bone taken from a canyon in Montana. She was shocked to discover soft, pliable tissue inside the bone!

Later analysis revealed that it contained red blood cells and the unique hemoglobin protein, which deteriorates very rapidly. Surely if dinosaurs died millions of years ago, any trace of this protein would be long gone.

50 um

A petroleum geologist working in Alaska in 1967 discovered a large bed of bones. Since the bones were fresh, he assumed that these were deposited recently. Twenty years later, some scientists recognized duckbilled and horned dinosaur bones in this deposit.[10]

Creationist adventurer Buddy Davis participated with a team that traveled to the North Slope in Alaska where they investigated the Liscomb Bone Bed. They discovered thousands of frozen dinosaur bones that appear to be unfossilized (some of them from a Lambeosaurus) with tail bone tendons still attached.[11] This does not fit the evolutionary story of dinosaurs becoming extinct 60 million years ago.

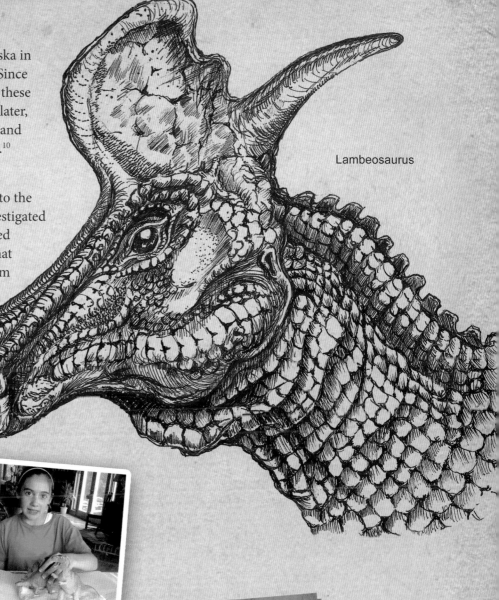

Lambeosaurus

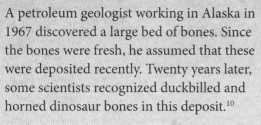

## Make a Fossil

Mix 4 cups of all-purpose flour, 1 cup of salt, and 1½ cups of water in a bowl.

Slowly add more water if needed till a thick dough is formed. Place on a cookie sheet and make impressions in it or form it into shapes. Then bake at 350 degrees for about an hour (depending on thickness).

What you are doing is quite similar to the way real fossils were created. Plants and animals left impressions in the soft mud, which later hardened into rock. Much of what we know about ancient, extinct animals and plants comes from such fossils. That is how we know about dinosaur skin, for example.

Fossilized shell

33

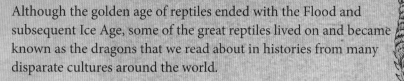

Although the golden age of reptiles ended with the Flood and subsequent Ice Age, some of the great reptiles lived on and became known as the dragons that we read about in histories from many disparate cultures around the world.

How did many ancient civilizations, that never interacted, come to believe in dragons? *The World Book Encyclopedia* notes, "The dragons of legend are strangely like actual creatures that have lived in the past. They are much like the great reptiles which inhabited the earth long before man is supposed to have appeared on earth. Dragons were generally evil and destructive. Every country had them in its mythology."[12]

The fathers of modern paleontology used the terms "dragon" and "dinosaur" interchangeably. Familiarity with dragons persisted through the Middle Ages and up into the 17th century. This might be called the historical era of the great reptiles. Doubtless, some of the dragon stories that have been handed down over the generations have been exaggerated through the years. But that does not mean they had no original basis in fact. Even the atheistic astronomer Carl Sagan once remarked: "The pervasiveness of dragon myths in the folk legends of many cultures is probably no accident."[13] Sagan speculated that these myths came from vestigial memories passed down from our ancient mammalian ancestors who saw the dinosaurs!

## Dragon-Dinosaur Fossil

In 2004, a fascinating dinosaur skull was donated to the Children's Museum of Indianapolis by three Sioux City, Iowa, residents who found it during a trip to the Hell Creek Formation in South Dakota. The trio is still excavating the site, looking for more of the dinosaur's bones. Because of its dragon-like head, horns, and teeth, the new species was dubbed Dracorex hogwartsia. This name honors the Harry Potter fictional works, which features the Hogwarts School, and recently popularized dragons. The dinosaur's skull mixes spiky horns, bumps, and a long muzzle, reminiscent of some of the features of dragon depictions.

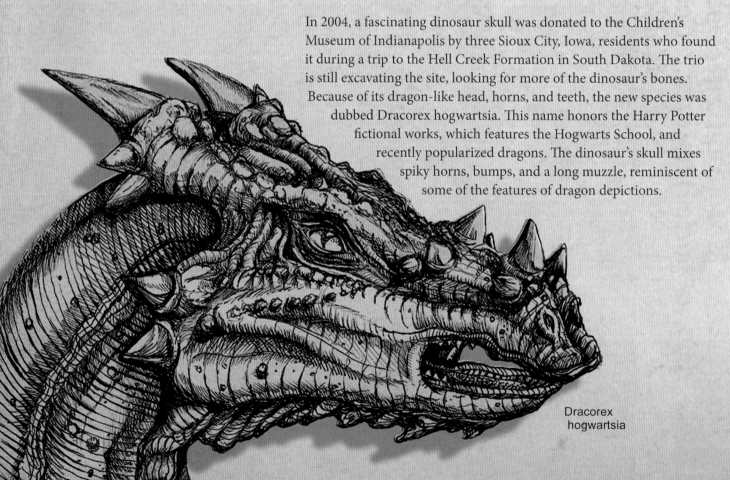

Dracorex
hogwartsia

# Dinosaur-Like Dragon Reports

Dragons are featured as far back as the ancient *Gilgamesh Epic*, a Sumerian story written about 2000 B.C. After Alexander the Great invaded India he brought back reports of seeing a great hissing dragon living in a cave. Later, Greek rulers supposedly captured dragons in Ethiopia and brought them back alive.

The Chinese have many stories of dragons. Some of their ornamental pictures of dragons display features remarkably like dinosaurs. Marco Polo wrote of his travels to the province of Karajan and reported on huge serpents, which at the fore part have two short legs, each with three claws and large jaws.[14]

Books even tell of Chinese families raising dragons to use their blood for medicines and highly prizing their eggs. It is interesting that the 12 signs of the Chinese zodiac are all animals — 11 of which are still alive today. But is the 12th, the dragon, merely a legend or is it based on a real animal —the dinosaur?

It doesn't seem logical that the ancient Chinese, when constructing their zodiac, would include one mythical animal with 11 real animals. Authorities on Chinese history have traced the interpretation of dinosaurs as dragons back more than two thousand years in their culture.[15]

Crylophosaurus

35

## Dragon of Carthage

St. John of Damascus, an eastern monk who wrote in the eighth century, gives a sober account of dragons, insisting that they are mere reptiles and did not have magical powers. He quotes the Roman historian Dio who wrote concerning the Roman empire in the second century. Regulus, a Roman consul, fought against Carthage, when a dragon suddenly crept up and settled behind the wall of the Roman army. The Romans killed it, skinned it, and sent the hide to the Roman senate. Dio claimed the hide was measured by order of the senate and found to be 120 feet long. It seems unlikely that either Dio or the pious St. John would support an outright fabrication involving a Roman consul and the senate.

St. John of Damascus

## Aldrovandus' Dragon

Ulysses Aldrovandus is considered by many to be the father of modern natural history. He traveled extensively, collected thousands of animals and plants, and created the first ever natural history museum. His impressive collections are today housed in a special wing at the Bologna University, where they attest to his scholarship. I give this background to give credence to the following incident that Aldrovandus personally reported concerning a dragon.

Ulysses Aldrovandus

The dragon was first seen on May 13, 1572, hissing like a snake. He had been hiding on the small estate of Master Petronius near Dosius in a place called Malonolta. At 5 p.m., he was caught on a public highway by a herdsman named Baptista of Camaldulus, near the hedge of a private farm, a mile from the remote city outskirts of Bologna. Baptista was following his ox cart home when he noticed the oxen suddenly come to a stop.

He kicked them and shouted at them, but they refused to move and went down on their knees rather than move forward. At this point, the herdsman noticed a hissing sound and was startled to see this strange little dragon ahead of him. Trembling, he struck it on the head with his rod and killed it.[16]

Aldrovandus identified it as a reptile, the first of this type that he had seen. The strange creature seemed to be completely harmless. Aldrovandus surmised that dragon was a juvenile, judging by the incompletely developed claws and teeth. The corpse had only two feet. It moved both by slithering like a snake and by using its feet, he believed. (There are small two-legged lizards that do this today.) Aldrovandus mounted the specimen and displayed it for some time. He also had a watercolor painting of the creature made. I had the privilege of personally viewing Aldrovandus' impressive mounts, including a lizard and a crocodilian. It is regrettable that, while these all nicely survived, the dragon mount has disappeared.

The familiar story of Beowulf and the legend of Saint George slaying a dragon, which are well known in the annals of English literature, likely have some basis in fact. Indeed the "dragon" pictured below is the dinosaur Baryonyx, whose skeleton has been found in England. Dragons were even described in reputable zoological treatises published during the Middle Ages. For example, the great Swiss naturalist and medical doctor Konrad Gesner published a four-volume encyclopedia from 1516–1565 entitled *Historiae Animalium*. He mentioned dragons as "very rare but still living creatures."

Konrad Gesner

Saint George and the Dragon — one of the most common dragon motifs through Medieval Europe

# Pterosaur-Like Dragon Reports

The ancient Jewish historian Josephus told of small flying reptiles in ancient Egypt and Arabia and described how the predatory ibis bird halted their invasion into Egypt. The well-respected Greek researcher Herodotus wrote: "There is a place in Arabia, situated very near the city of Buto, to which I went, on hearing of some winged serpents; and when I arrived there, I saw bones and spines of serpents, in such quantities as it would be impossible to describe. The form of the serpent is like that of the water-snake; but he has wings without feathers, and as like as possible to the wings of a bat."[17]

Josephus

This is a remarkable description of a pterosaur. In his third volume, Herodotus goes on to tell how these animals could sometimes be found in the Arabian spice groves. He describes their size, coloration, and reproduction. It seems flying serpents were infamous for hanging in frankincense trees. When workers wanted to gather the tree's incense, they would employ putrid smoke to drive the flying reptiles away.

The ancient authors Aristotle, Aelianus, Ammianus, Mela, Solinus, Matthew of Edessa, Cicero, and Philae all reference flying serpents.

Herodotus

Medieval eyewitnesses say this iridescent
"winged serpent" had every color of the rainbow.

Reliable witness reports of "flying dragons" (pterosaur-like creatures) in Europe were written around 1649. Marie Trevelyan records, "The woods around Penllyn Castle, Glamorgan, had the reputation of being frequented by winged serpents, and these were the terror of old and young alike. An aged inhabitant of Penllyn, who died a few years ago, said that in his boyhood the winged serpents were described as very beautiful. They were coiled when in repose, and 'looked as if they were covered with jewels of all sorts. Some of them had crests sparkling with all the colours of the rainbow.' When disturbed they glided swiftly, 'sparkling all over,' to their hiding places."[18]

The prolific 17th-century writer Athanasius Kircher tells how the noble man, Christopher Schorerum, prefect of the entire territory, witnessed a phenomenon, written in his own words: "On a warm night in 1619, while contemplating the serenity of the heavens, I saw a shining dragon of great size in front of Mt. Pilatus, coming from the opposite side of the lake, a cave that is named Flue moving rapidly in an agitated way, seen flying across;

It was of a large size, with a long tail, a long neck, a reptile's head, and ferocious gaping jaws. As it flew it was like iron struck in a forge when pressed together that scatters sparks. At first I thought it was a meteor from what I saw. But after I diligently observed it alone, I understood it was indeed a dragon from the motion of the limbs of the entire body."[19]

**Athanasius Kircher**

# Plesiosaur-Like Dragon Reports

In medieval times, the Scandinavians described swimming dragons and the Vikings placed carved dragons on the front of their ships to scare off the sea monsters. Hans Egede, missionary to Greenland, was known to keep a meticulous recording of natural observations. His account of a "sea monster" he saw off the coast in 1734 is the basis for the drawing to the right.

A well-publicized sea serpent sighting was made by the men and officers of HMS Daedalus in August of 1848. The monster they saw measured approximately 60 feet long and sported a mane on its head. Numerous other such stories have been recorded from the great age of sailing ships (A.D. 1500–1900) when men traversed the ocean without the noise of modern powered vessels.

The evidence is compelling that some of the great reptiles survived near populated areas and were known as dragons. Evolutionary zoologist Desmond Morris conceded, "In the world of fantastic animals, the dragon is unique. . . . It is as though there was once a whole family of different dragon species that really existed, before they mysteriously became extinct.

THE GREAT SEA SERPENT
( according to Hans Egede )

Indeed, as recently as the 17th century, scholars wrote of dragons as though they were scientific fact, their anatomy and natural history being recorded in painstaking detail."[20]

But by the 19th century, dragons had largely been wiped out by expanding civilizations. Men viewed them as a threat and hunted them down, both to secure new lands for settlement and to prove their dominance. The changing ecosystems and rise of colonial empires drove many species, including most of the dragons, into extinction. And so ended the historical age of the great reptiles.

Oseberg Viking ship head post in the Viking Ship Museum, Oslo, Norway

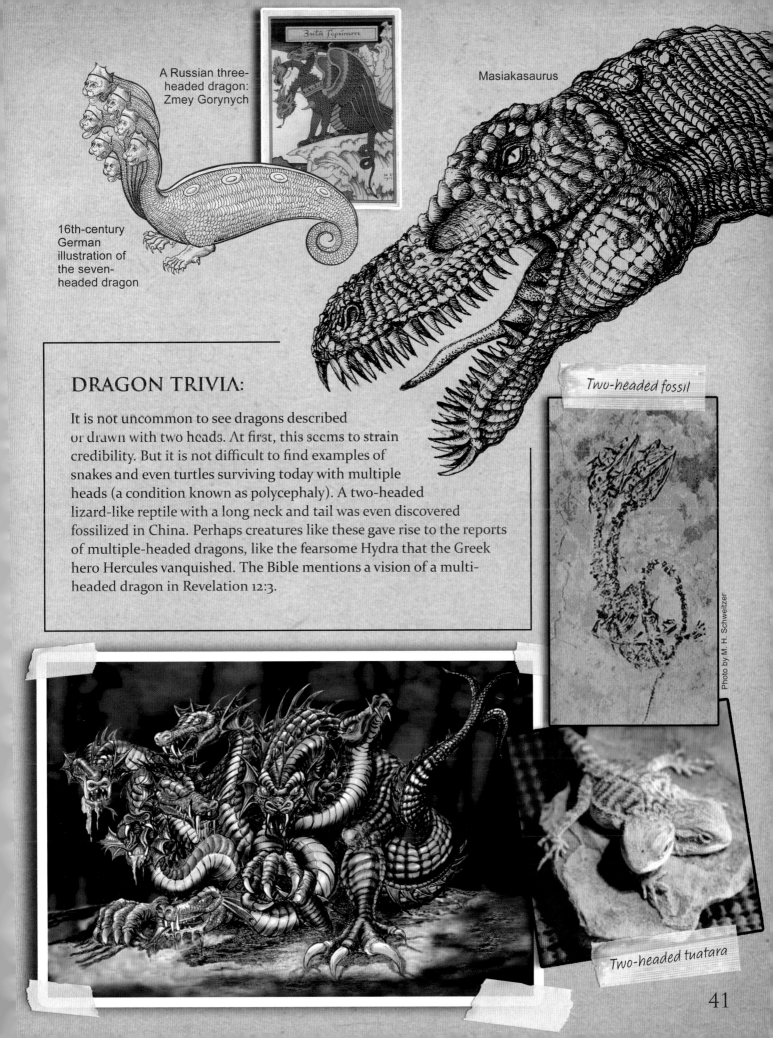

A Russian three-headed dragon: Zmey Gorynych

Masiakasaurus

16th-century German illustration of the seven-headed dragon

## DRAGON TRIVIA:

It is not uncommon to see dragons described or drawn with two heads. At first, this seems to strain credibility. But it is not difficult to find examples of snakes and even turtles surviving today with multiple heads (a condition known as polycephaly). A two-headed lizard-like reptile with a long neck and tail was even discovered fossilized in China. Perhaps creatures like these gave rise to the reports of multiple-headed dragons, like the fearsome Hydra that the Greek hero Hercules vanquished. The Bible mentions a vision of a multi-headed dragon in Revelation 12:3.

Two-headed fossil

Photo by M. H. Schweitzer

Two-headed tuatara

41

# CHAPTER 5

# Artistic Evidence
# of Dinosaurs and Man

Along with the numerous historical accounts of dragons that have come down to us from antiquity, there are many ancient artistic works depicting the great reptiles as men knew them. There is only space to discuss a small percentage of these artifacts in this scrapbook. In almost all of these cases, the ancient artist is unknown. Yet the similarities between the iconography and known kinds of dinosaurs is striking evidence that these artists saw or heard reliable reports of the great reptiles in their day.

## ARTWORK FROM SOUTH AMERICA

In the 1500s, the Spanish conquistadors brought back stories that there were Ica ceremonial stones with strange creatures carved on them found in Peru. Some of the stones were later carried to Spain and their existence was recorded by the Incan chronicler Pachacuti-Yamqui in 1571. A direct descendant of a conquistador, Dr. Javier Cabrera, saw these stones as a child and began collecting them in the 1960s. Today, over 11,000 such Ica stones have been found, some depicting dinosaurs. Upon retiring from the University of Lima, Cabrera worked to validate these finds within the scientific community. His credibility was strengthened by the discovery of pottery (now in a Lima museum) and tapestry found in the tombs (dated from A.D. 200–700) that display similar creatures. Indeed, the depictions on some of the Ica stones show sauropod dinosaurs with a crest of spines much like that discovered on fossilized skin impressions by paleontologist Stephen Czerkas.[21] Moreover, the skin of many of the carved dinosaurs has rounded bump-like depictions. Some scientists had pointed to this as evidence that these stones were not scientifically accurate. However, discoveries of fossilized dinosaur skin and certain sauropod dinosaur embryos found in South America display round, non-overlapping, tubercle-like scales in a rosette pattern that has silenced these critics.

Photos by Dennis Swift

Not far from the South American Nazca sites are the Moche Indian archaeological locations. These Moche tribes inhabited northern Peru from about A.D. 100 to 800.

Among the artifacts currently in the Rafael Larco Herrera Museum are the Moche stirrup-spout pots and vases.

Their main artistic medium was the red and white ceramic pots, which depict with singular realism long-necked dinosaurs with three and sometimes four toes. Some of these same types of dinosaurs are shown on the Ica stones, sporting the same dermal frills.

Photos by Dennis Swift.

## DINO DRAWING EXPERIMENT:

See how accurately you can redraw from memory. Carefully look at a particular dinosaur in the scrapbook. Close the book and try to draw it from memory. How close does your drawing resemble the original? Now try this. Choose an unfamiliar kind of dinosaur and try explaining it in detail to a friend. Without letting him see the picture, have your friend attempt to draw it. Now, how close did that picture come to the original? This exercise helps us understand how difficult it was for ancient artists to accurately draw dragons from memory or first-hand reports.

Iguanodon incorrectly drawn from fossil evidence in 1822

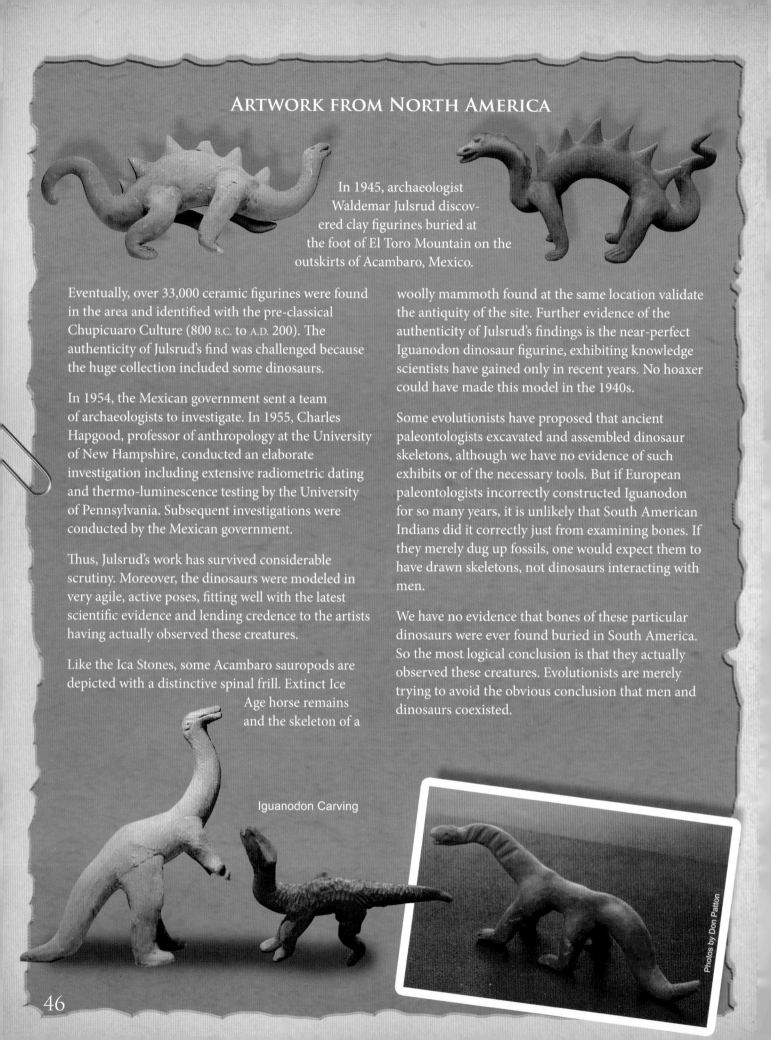

# ARTWORK FROM NORTH AMERICA

In 1945, archaeologist Waldemar Julsrud discovered clay figurines buried at the foot of El Toro Mountain on the outskirts of Acambaro, Mexico.

Eventually, over 33,000 ceramic figurines were found in the area and identified with the pre-classical Chupicuaro Culture (800 B.C. to A.D. 200). The authenticity of Julsrud's find was challenged because the huge collection included some dinosaurs.

In 1954, the Mexican government sent a team of archaeologists to investigate. In 1955, Charles Hapgood, professor of anthropology at the University of New Hampshire, conducted an elaborate investigation including extensive radiometric dating and thermo-luminescence testing by the University of Pennsylvania. Subsequent investigations were conducted by the Mexican government.

Thus, Julsrud's work has survived considerable scrutiny. Moreover, the dinosaurs were modeled in very agile, active poses, fitting well with the latest scientific evidence and lending credence to the artists having actually observed these creatures.

Like the Ica Stones, some Acambaro sauropods are depicted with a distinctive spinal frill. Extinct Ice Age horse remains and the skeleton of a woolly mammoth found at the same location validate the antiquity of the site. Further evidence of the authenticity of Julsrud's findings is the near-perfect Iguanodon dinosaur figurine, exhibiting knowledge scientists have gained only in recent years. No hoaxer could have made this model in the 1940s.

Some evolutionists have proposed that ancient paleontologists excavated and assembled dinosaur skeletons, although we have no evidence of such exhibits or of the necessary tools. But if European paleontologists incorrectly constructed Iguanodon for so many years, it is unlikely that South American Indians did it correctly just from examining bones. If they merely dug up fossils, one would expect them to have drawn skeletons, not dinosaurs interacting with men.

We have no evidence that bones of these particular dinosaurs were ever found buried in South America. So the most logical conclusion is that they actually observed these creatures. Evolutionists are merely trying to avoid the obvious conclusion that men and dinosaurs coexisted.

Iguanodon Carving

Photos by Don Patton

The petroglyph to the right was created by North American Anasazi Indians that lived in the area that has now become Utah from approximately 150 B.C. to A.D. 1200. Even noted anti-creationists agree that it resembles a dinosaur and that the brownish film that has hardened over the picture, along with the pitting and weathering, attests to its age. Clearly, a native warrior and an apatosaur-like creature are depicted.

Henry Rowe Schoolcraft was a geologist and Indian agent who wrote extensively about the Sioux Indians. He heard stories about a monstrous creature called Unktehi — something like an ox but much larger, with great horns.

Schoolcraft reproduced drawings of several types of Unktehi monsters around 1850. These were based upon rock art showing a war party of five canoes crossing Lake Superior that encountered animals resembling giant turtles, snakes, and moose. But some (middle right) clearly look dinosaurian. Sioux Indians farther west, when interviewed by ethnologists, described Unktehi as an immense reptile or serpent with legs. Its shape was like a giant scaly snake with feet, with a notched backbone or crest, and a heavy, spiked tail. Still other Indian reports describe Unktehi as a swamp-dwelling creature.

Henry Rowe Schoolcraft

The pictures and description bring to mind the dinosaur Ankylosaurus with a low-slung body, long tail, heavy armor, and prominent multiple horns. A similar plated and horned creature has also been discovered in Cree Indian art (right) on the Agawa Rock at Misshepezhieu, Lake Superior Provincial Park, Ontario, Canada.

Ankylosaur

# ARTWORK FROM ASIA

Asian stylized dragon depictions are fairly common. But some bear a remarkable resemblance to known types of dinosaurs. Consider the dragon statue to the right, which has been authenticated by an industrial x-ray specialist. The bronze styling on this artifact suggests it is at least as old as the Han Dynasty (206 B.C.–A.D. 220). It displays numerous characteristics of the beaked dinosaurs (like the Oviraptor): tridactyl feet configuration, metatarsal stance, scale-like representation all over the body (except for the horn, which has a striated pattern), long (albeit slender) tail, elaborate head crests, and a long neck.

Another fascinating Chinese artifact (middle right), from the Shang Dynasty (1766–1122 B.C.), is a dragon that displays relief lines in a scale-like pattern, a broad beak, a dermal frill, and a head crest that is strikingly like the dinosaur Saurolophus. This jade statue is made of white colored nephrite with differential weathering, cleaving veins, and earth penetration, demonstrating authenticity. Lastly, notice the beautiful Hongshan bloodstone carving (made about 4,000 years ago). This dragon bears an astonishing resemblance to a small Protoceratops dinosaur.

Deep in the jungles of Cambodia are ornate temples and palaces from the Khmer civilization. One such temple, Ta Prohm, abounds with stone statues and reliefs. Almost every square inch of the grey sandstone is covered with ornate, detailed carvings. These depict familiar animals like monkeys, deer, water buffalo, parrots, and lizards. However, one column contains an intricate carving of a stegosaur-like creature. But how could artisans decorating an 800-year-old Buddhist temple know what a dinosaur looked like? Western science only began assembling dinosaurs skeletons in the past two centuries.

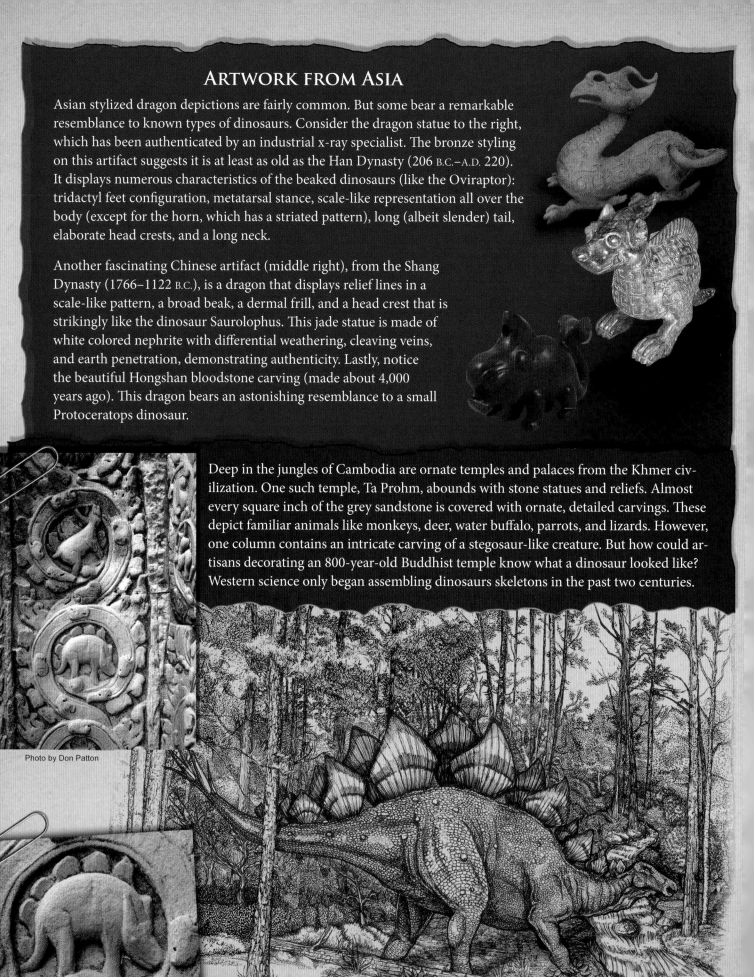

Photo by Don Patton

# Artwork from the Middle East

To the left is an urn from Caria (modern Turkey), estimated to be from 530 B.C. It depicts what appears to be a mosasaurus. The animal behind the sea monster is a seal, while an octopus is below, along with what seems to be a dolphin. The thick jaws, big teeth, large eyes, and positioning of the flippers on this creature match a mosasaurus skeleton very well.

Uruk Seal

Art from a Mesopotamian cylinder seal of Uruk dated to about 3000 B.C., and is currently housed at the Louvre (see right). There is a striking resemblance to modern artists' renditions of the Apatosaurus. The legs and feet on the artifact clearly fit the sauropods better than any other type of animal. The only odd feature is at the head. Cartilage forming the shape of a frill or ears may be stylized or accurate (since there is no way to know from skeletons). The ancient artist depicted the musculature with stunning realism. One has to ask where the artist got the model to draw the neck of a dinosaur so convincingly.

Cosmetic palettes from ancient Egypt also show long-necked creatures that fit this same pattern, including arching, muscular necks, and stout bodies. To the right are displayed slate palettes from Hierakonpolis showing the triumph of King Narmer with long-necked dragons and an ancient palette depicting a pair of "dinosaur-like" creatures along with numerous clear representations of living animals. An Egyptian magical wand (made from a hippo tusk) dates to about 1750 B.C. and displays a similar long-necked creature.

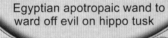

Egyptian apotropaic wand to ward off evil on hippo tusk

Image credit: British Museum

This long-necked animal motif is so common in ancient Middle Eastern art that archaeologists who do not believe that men and dinosaurs coexisted have dubbed it a "serpopard" (a composite of a serpent and a leopard). But all of the other animals on these palettes are quite realistically drawn. It is far more reasonable to believe that man was created in the beginning alongside the great reptiles. These palettes seem to be an attempt to depict a sauropod dinosaur.

In 600 B.C., under the reign of King Nebuchadnezzar, a Babylonian artist was commissioned to shape reliefs of animals on the structures associated with

the Ishtar Gate. The animals appear in alternating rows with lions, fierce bulls, and curious long-necked dragons. No doubt this is the same creature that is referenced in the apocryphal account of Daniel, the idol Bel, and the dragon. Archaeologist Robert Koldewey discovered the gate in 1902 and he believed that the "sirrush" (above) was a portrayal of a real animal.

## Artwork from Africa

The Ashanti people of Ghana in western Africa are known for their carvings that were used over the centuries as gold weights. Many are little statues that accurately depict various African animals. The curious gold weight to the left, now part of the Penn Museum collection (Object #234234, Image #AF2478), was identified back in the 1960s as resembling a juvenile dinosaur.[22] It has a fan tail and a beak-like mouth, distinctive characteristics of some of the recently discovered oviraptorosaurs.

## Artwork from Europe

It was popular during the Roman Empire to decorate walls and especially floors with mosaics (art composed of many small glazed tiles). On the top of the following page is the beautiful Nile Mosaic (dated to approximately 100 B.C.), currently housed in a museum in Palestrina, Italy.

It depicts African scenes from Egypt all the way to Ethiopia. The top portion of this remarkable piece of art shows African animals being hunted by black-skinned warriors. The Ethiopians are pursuing what appears to be some type of dinosaur. The classical block Greek letters above the reptilian animal in question are KROKODILOPARDALIS, which is literally translated "crocodile-leopard," designating an agile reptilian creature. The massive mosaic also presents clear depictions of known animals, including Egyptian crocodiles and hippos.

Another fascinating mosaic was discovered at Lydney Park in Gloucestershire, England. It dates back to about A.D. 400. The surviving fragments depict dolphins, fish, and two long-necked sea dragons. Creationist Paul Taylor likens them to the web-footed Tanystropheus, a swimming reptile presumed extinct.[23]

Tanystropheus fossil

ΚΡΟΚΟΔΙΛΟΠΑΡΔΑΛΙC

Close-up of Nile Mosaic dinosaur

Tanystropheus on seashore

Nile Mosaic

Plateosaurus

# European Medieval Decorations

Some of the beautiful French chateaus built at the close of the Middle Ages and early 1500s have dramatic dragon illustrations carved into their walls, ceilings, and furniture. These include Château de Chambord, de Blois, and Azay-le-Rideau. Note the similarities between these creatures and dinosaurs like Plateosaurus.

The Château Azay-le-Rideau also displays a fascinating tapestry depicting what looks like a pterosaur fighting a lion. Another tapestry at Château de Blois portrays a dragon and its baby.

Lion fights pterosaur

Dragon and baby

The slaying of a ferocious dragon by St. George is an extremely common motif in medieval art. Various European artists interpreted the dragon differently, depending on local knowledge and lore. A wonderful 15th century depiction is seen in the chapel at the Palau de La Generalitat in Barcelona, Spain. Vance Nelson points out that the altar cloth bears an amazing likeness to a Nothosaurus, a semi-aquatic reptile (shown below).[24] Notice the correct size, the crocodilian body shape, and the fascinating curved teeth at the front of the jaw that gives way to smaller, fine dentition toward the throat.

Nothosaurus

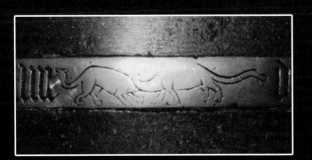

In 1496 the Bishop of Carlisle, Richard Bell, was buried in Carlisle Cathedral in the United Kingdom. The tomb is inlaid with brass, with various animals engraved upon it. Although worn by countless feet since the Middle Ages, a particular depiction is remarkable in its similarity to a dinosaur. Among the birds, dog, eel, etc., this clear representation of two long-necked creatures should be considered evidence that man and dinosaurs coexisted.

To the right is a fascinating depiction of a flying serpent from the ceiling of the San Miniato al Monte church in Florence, Italy, built in the 11th century. Notice the beak, four claws on the foot, head crest, coiled tail, and bat-like wings. These are all distinctive characteristics of pterosaurs. Note as well the reptilian forked tongue.

A dragon was said to have lived in a cave near some wetlands not far from Rome. This creature supposedly terrorized the local population and was killed in December of 1691. A sketch of the skeleton survived through the years (left). A most remarkable detail is the clear head crest with dual pieces of skin. Five digits are clearly visible on each foot and the specimen fits the proportions of the pterosaur Scaphognathus. There is a hint of a wing claw on the far wing where it curves forward. The membrane wings are in front of the legs, on the correct vertebrae, matching the fossils. The femur is properly shown as a single bone. The tibia and fibula, the twin lower leg bones, are visible, too. Skeptics suggested that it could be an assembled fossil or a faked composite. But it is much too accurate to be a fabrication and the survival of the skin suggests that it is not a fossil since it includes accurate wing features, a head crest, and the ears.

In 1704, *Hœllischer Morpheus* was published, featuring information on the black arts. Because the Bible referred to Satan as "that old dragon," multiple flying serpents are depicted in the book. On the frontispiece of the work is a clear depiction of a pterosaur, represented with two feet, wings, and a snake-like tail ending in a tail vane.

Another pterosaur-like depiction (lower left) from the Middle Ages is shown in Athanasius Kircher's 1678 book *Mundus Subterraneus*. This drawing is so compelling that Peter Wellnhofer (who wrote *The Illustrated Encyclopedia of Pterosaurs*) suggested it might have been based on fossil finds.[25] But it is more likely based on even more ancient reports. While the erect wings (rather than tucked down on the body like a bird) are distinctively pterosaur-like, the fore-limbs are not correctly incorporated into the wing. Kircher also includes a picture of a dragon (below) that resembles the rhamphorhynchoid pterosaurs.

A 1971 landslide in the Girifalco region of southern Italy brought to light hundreds of ancient artifacts of a pre-Greek civilization. A lawyer named Mario Tolone Azzariti asserts that he found some dinosaurian representations among them. Shown below is a terracotta statue, shaped remarkably like a Stegosaurus, with triangular plates going down its back. In the view from above (lower left) the object reveals a curious curving of the plates, as if representing the creature in an undulating motion. The legs are large and awkward, as if carrying great weight, not at all like those of a lizard. A clear profile of a Stegosaurus was also discovered on a piece of bro-ken pottery (upper right).[26]

# CHURCH ORNAMENTATION

Choir stall railings and misericords (shelf-like seats for reclining while standing) in medieval European churches are often adorned with ornate carvings. A common theme is the depiction of a dragon (symbolizing Satan) fighting a lion (symbolizing Christ). To the right is one such depiction, showing a dragon that looks very much like a sauropod dinosaur, taken from St. Remigius' Church. The other pictures are taken from Carlisle Cathedral's misericords, carved in the 15th century.

San Zan Degolà is a beautiful little 13th-century church in Venice, Italy. It has a wonderfully preserved fresco depicting the archangel Michael overcoming the dragon (a common Medieval image taken from Revelation 20:1–2). The dragons proportions and its small front legs bring to mind the small theropod dinosaurs.

Compsognathus silhouette

---

# ARTWORK FROM AUSTRALIA

There are stories of a plesiosaur-like creature seen in North Queensland, Australia. Both aboriginal peoples around Lake Galilee and tribes farther up to the north tell of a long-necked animal with a large body and flippers. Elders relate stories of the creature, Yarru, which used to inhabit rain forest water holes. An indigenous painting depicts a creature with features remarkably like a plesiosaur. It even shows a realistic outline of the gastrointestinal tract, suggesting that these animals had been hunted and butchered.

57

Today it is assumed that all of the great reptiles are extinct. Almost every magazine article, book, museum exhibit, or park display that mentions dinosaurs, plesiosaurs, or pterosaurs begins with an opening paragraph referencing "millions and millions of years ago. . . ." But the world is a big place and there are plenty of remote locations that have not been thoroughly explored. The area of scientific research that investigates reports and rumors of undiscovered animals is called cryptozoology. Until a living or recently deceased specimen is validated, we can't speak definitively to any of the great reptiles existing today. We live in the cryptozoology age of dinosaurs.

## Cryptozoology

The term "cryptozoology" was first used in a 1959 book by Lucien Blancou. It was later popularized by zoologist Bernard Heuvelmans. The term has now become a standard part of modern vocabulary and appears in almost all dictionaries. It is defined as "the science of hidden animals."

Monitor lizard

There are a number of species that were thought to be extinct that have been found in recent history. Some of these formerly "hidden creatures" (cryptids) include the megamouth shark and the coelacanth fish. New species are still being discovered fairly regularly in remote places like Papua New Guinea and the Amazon basin of South America.

Usually these discoveries involve plants and small animals. But in 2009, as a result of an intense effort, a six-foot-long monitor lizard was found, photographed, and classified as a new species in the Philippines.

A cryptozoologist is someone who systematically seeks to track down species or sub-species that are still unknown to science. There are a number of remote regions where intriguing reports give cryptozoologists hope of finding a dinosaurian cryptid!

Coelocanth

# Ceratopsian in Africa

The remote swamps of central Africa would seem to be the ideal place to find a dinosaurian creature still lurking. One of the cryptids said to inhabit the massive swamps of the Congo is the Emela-ntouka (literally "killer of elephants").

This stout rhinoceros-like creature is reputed to have a penchant for killing elephants with its single horn. Lucien Blancou, chief game inspector in French Equatorial Africa in the 1950s, wrote of a ferocious creature in the Congo, larger than a buffalo, that was considered the most dangerous animal by the Kelle pygmies, ". . . the presence of a beast which sometimes disembowels elephants is also known, but it does not seem to be prevalent there now as in the preceding districts. A specimen was supposed to have been killed 20 years ago at Dongou, but on the left of the Ubangi and in the Belgian Congo."[27]

A number of other African explorers have written of the mysterious monster that gores elephants with its single horn. Explorer Roy Mackal speculated that the Emela-ntouka was a Centrosaurus.[28] This member of the Ceratopsian family (formerly the Monoclonius) sports a single large horn at the center of its head. The ceratopsian identification has been strengthened by similar reports that I obtained during my November 2000 expedition into the swamps of Cameroon. In 2004, the French cryptozoologist Michel Ballot photographed a native wood carving (upper right) of this fascinating cryptid.

# Mokele-Mbembe of Africa

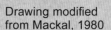

Drawing modified from Mackal, 1980

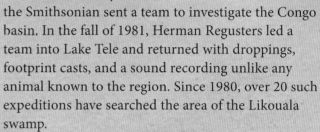

In November of 1980 the readers of the popular magazine *Science-80* were presented with the following sensational report entitled "Living Dinosaurs":

> *In the swampy jungles of western Africa, reports persist of an elephant-sized creature with smooth, brownish-gray skin, a long, flexible neck, a very long tail as powerful as a crocodile's, and three-clawed feet the size of frying pans. Over the past three centuries, native Pygmies and Western explorers have told how the animals feed on the nutlike fruit of a riverbank plant and keep to the deep pools and subsurface caves of waters in this largely unexplored region. After a recent expedition there, two American researchers conclude that these stories refer to a real animal, not a myth. Fantastic as it seems, Roy Mackal [University of Chicago] and James Powell believe that this creature, called "Mokele-Mbembe" by the natives, may actually be a dinosaur, perhaps one resembling brontosaurus, which is thought to have died out 70 million years ago.*[29]

The forbidding Likouala swamp region, located in the northern part of the Congo, is about the size of the state of Arkansas. It was not until missionaries showed Congolese natives a sauropod dinosaur that they identified this mysterious animal living in the rivers and deep swamp pools. A vegetarian, the creature will fight with hippos over a territory rich in molombo plants. Reports of Mokele-Mbembe go all the way back to the 18th century. In 1919, the Smithsonian sent a team to investigate the Congo basin. In the fall of 1981, Herman Regusters led a team into Lake Tele and returned with droppings, footprint casts, and a sound recording unlike any animal known to the region. Since 1980, over 20 such expeditions have searched the area of the Likouala swamp.

In the fall of 2000, Bill Gibbons and I led an expedition to pioneer research in southeastern Cameroon (along the Congo border) by slogging through swamps, floating jungle rivers, trekking virgin rain forests, and interviewing pygmy forest peoples who had never before talked to an outside explorer. From village to village, informants recognized the same hippo-sized sauropod creature known in the Congo and selected it from a lineup of various animals.

Eyewitnesses led us to places where it had been seen, in some cases quite recently. Its actions were described in fascinating detail and in harmony with Dr. Mackal's information from the Congo research. We learned how it jealously guards its section of the river, even against ferocious crocodiles and hippos, by lashing its enemies with its tail!

A follow-up trip to Cameroon was initiated by the BBC in 2001. Yet another expedition, led by Canadian Brian Sass, discovered an island in the Dja River which contained nesting caves like those identified by Mackal. Casts of footprints and photographs of the nests were obtained. Sass actually had a brief encounter with the elusive monster as a Mokele-Mbembe swam past his dugout canoe toward its lair. Subsequent investigation has been carried out by the French researcher Michel Ballot and further expeditions are planned.

Cameroon expedition 2000

Photo by Roy Mackel

# Sea Serpents And Swimming Monsters

The least-explored region of the earth is the deep ocean. Over the years, reports have circulated of monstrous swimming creatures, sighted at sea and in some very deep lakes. Numerous historical reports involve an elongated, serpentine form unknown in the fossil record. But some curious characteristics of the monsters in these accounts include a neck frill, fluke-like tail, a body that can flex into humps, and flippers. Note the ancient mosaic and the drawing from 1639 based on a credible sea serpent sighting in Cape Ann off the Massachusetts coast. Zoologist Karl Shuker speculated that some of these encounters might have involved a still-living Basilosaurus, a slender whale-like creature supposed to have been extinct for millions of years.[30] It possessed small fins and a flexible neck and could undulate its long body vertically (unlike known snakes that coil horizontally).

Sea serpent in Cape Ann, 1639

Probably the most-respected "sea serpent" story involves the Cadborosaurus ("Caddy"), which has been observed numerous times off the coast of British Columbia (especially around Cadboro Bay, from which it gets its name). The Native Americans of the Pacific Northwest have legends of a sea serpent that they depicted in rock carvings. Below is a tracing of a petroglyph from a large rock near Sproat Lake, in Vancouver Island, British Columbia. Professor Paul H. LeBlond of the University of British Columbia presented a compelling paper on Caddy to the Canadian and American Societies of Zoology, highlighting the picture of a ten-foot carcass of an apparent juvenile (bottom) that was discovered in the stomach of a sperm whale.[31]

Sonar images from the
Academy of Applied Sciences

Sonar photo from the Royal Scot

Author observing
at Loch Ness

## Loch Ness

Loch Ness Monster is easily the best known cryptid in the swimming category. Hundreds of people through the years claim to have seen Nessie, the mysterious creature that inhabits the deep waters of Scotland's famous lake. The Loch's amazing depth (over 800 feet) surpasses that of the North Sea. Reports of a monster in the murky waters date back to the missionary St. Columba in A.D. 565. Unfortunately, all of the famous pictures of Nessie are also highly disputed. Some of the best evidence are images taken utilizing sonar, which can penetrate the loch's dark, peaty waters like no other camera can. These include photos taken by the Academy of Applied Sciences which show what might be a creature's head and neck and a diamond-shaped flipper (top left pictures). When I visited Loch Ness during the summer of 2002, Skipper Ricky Macdonald of the *Royal Scot* displayed a sonar printout showing a very large creature passing under his boat. In the spring of 2012, another remarkable sonar encounter made headlines. Research continues and a new submarine search has begun. While no undisputed photographic evidence has been obtained, it has been said that many a person has been hanged on less evidence than we have of a monster existing in Loch Ness!

## Champ

In the summer of 1977, Sandra Mansi's family was relaxing on the shores of Lake Champlain. Suddenly she observed a monstrous creature surface about 150 feet offshore. After hurriedly getting her children in the car, Mansi took a historic photograph of the animal. Her account is the most complete and fully documented of any lake monster sighting. But many people, dating all the way back to the Abenaqi Indians, claim to have seen the creature called Champ. Lake Champlain lies on the border of New York and Vermont and is

The author at
Lake Champlain

accessed by sea through the St. Lawrence Seaway. The first recorded sighting took place when Samuel de Champlain came upon the lake in July 1609. During that expedition, the French explorer reported "a serpent-like creature about 20 feet long, as thick through as a barrel and with a head shaped like a horse."[32]

Since then, sightings of the strange aquatic beast have been reported by over 300 people, many chronicled by researcher Joseph Zarzynski. Underwater microphones installed in 2003 by a team doing research for the Discovery Channel picked up a high-pitched ticking and chirping noise in the lake, sounds similar to those made by a dolphin or a whale. Featured on the TV program *Unsolved Mysteries*, Champ has been amateur video-taped at least three times. On February 22, 2006, ABC News obtained an exclusive video of something just under the surface of the lake that seemed to be Champ. The video (which includes multiple humps and a long slender shape appearing to be a neck and head) was taken by two fishermen with their digital camera. Many people believe Champ to be a plesiosaur.

Photo by Sandra Mansi

# Ogopogo

Another deep lake that is said to harbor a mysterious creature is found in western North America. Lake Okanagan is the home of Ogopogo, a long serpent-like cryptid that has been rumored to live in caves far below the surface.

Researcher Arlene Gaal has compiled extensive reports, photos, and drawings of Ogopogo over the years. Reports predate the arrival of white men, for the Indians knew of the monster they called N'ha-a-itk and would bring along a small animal to sacrifice to the serpent in order to ensure safe passage. "With the arrival of the first settlers, stories of a large unknown animal in Okanagan Lake continued. Concerns arose and many settlers took turns patrolling the lakeshore, musket in hand, to protect their families from an impending Ogopogo attack."[33]

But most of the Ogopogo sightings have only involved a row of large humps, protruding out of the water. Some claim to have seen the creature's head and even observed it shooting water up like a fountain, similar to the ancient sea serpent reports. In July of 1989, a video was taken by Ken Chaplin showing the head of a large creature, an elongated body, and a tail that slapped the surface like a beaver.

Since some of the recorded observations involve the humps of the creature coming fully out of the water (like a hoop), it would seem like Ogopogo is closer in form to a serpent than a plesiosaur. Other stories about USO's (Unidentified Swimming Objects) abound from England, Sweden, Russia, France, Australia, Argentina, Japan, etc.

## AUTHOR SIGHTING

I personally saw the Ogopogo phenomenon from a boat in the summer of 2011. It occurred just off Ellison Provincial Park on a warm July evening. The lake had become very calm when all of the occupants of the boat plainly saw three dark humps in a line breaking the surface and then traveling off rapidly as they submerged again, leaving a huge wake behind them.

Ropen carving by an
unknown native artisan

# Ropen of Papua New Guinea

Duane Hodgkinson was stationed in PNG as part of the U.S. Army assigned to weather observation in 1944. One day he was walking up a trail and came to a grassy clearing in the forest when he was startled by a crashing in the brush. As he watched, a large bird-like creature ponderously rose from the ground, circled, and flew away. Hodgkinson, a pilot, estimated the wing-span to be about 20 feet. He clearly recalls the dark-gray coloration, long serpentine neck, beak, and distinctive head crest.

After the war, missionaries brought back additional reports of the creature nationals called the Ropen. The creature possesses leathery wings like a bat, a long tail with a flange on the end, a beak filled with teeth, and razor-sharp claws.

In October of 2004, Garth Guessman and I conducted a three-week trip to the remote Siassi Islands off the western coast of Papua New Guinea, somewhat south of Manus Island. Our team hiked into the mountainous interior of the volcanic Umboi Island to follow up on intriguing reports received from coastal communities on the south shore. Dozens of interviews were conducted and the credibility of witnesses was carefully tested by the use of black and white profiles. After carefully collating the dozens of interviews, a composite drawing

of likely characteristics possessed by the Ropen was assembled (below right).

The Ropen is said to be largely a nocturnal animal, having a 15- to 20-foot wingspan and producing a biolumi-nescent glow, like a firefly. On Wednesday, October 27, I observed a large, yel-lowish glow behind one of the volcanic peaks. The light left no trail and it twinkled around the edges. Most of the sightings by nationals involves this brief glowing phenomenon.

Modified from D.K. Images

At a hotel we photographed some intriguing carvings made by an unknown artisan. The statues show a medicine man with a reptilian creature on his shoulders (see above). The creatures have a lizard-like ear, forked tongue, elongated snake-like neck, shallow beak, scaly membrane wings, dermal bumps running down its back, webbed feet, and a long tail.

Follow-up expeditions led by Paul Nation and Destination Truth obtained the first video footage of a glowing Ropen's light as multiple creatures were observed flying together.

Pilot
Duane Hodgkinson

Native eyewitnesses
from the village of Arot

65

# CHAPTER 7
## Biblical Evidence of Dinosaurs and Man

Job 40:15-24

Behold now behemoth, which I made with thee; he eateth grass as an ox.
Lo now, his strength is in his loins, and his force is in the navel of his belly.
He moveth his tail like a cedar: the sinews of his stones are wrapped together.
His bones are as strong pieces of brass; his bones are like bars of iron.
He is the chief of the ways of God: he that made him can make his sword to approach unto him.
Surely the mountains bring him forth food, where all the beasts of the field play.
He lieth under the shady trees, in the covert of the reed, and fens.
The shady trees cover him with their shadow; the willows of the brook compass him about.

Megalania

There is no question that the straightforward, plain teaching of God's Word leads one to believe that dinosaurs and man coexisted. God Himself declared, "For in six days the LORD made heaven and earth, the sea, and all that in them is, and rested the seventh day" (Exodus 20:11). The pattern of God's literal six-day creation and Sabbath rest is an example for His followers to set aside a day of rest and worship every week. Not only were the dinosaurs created on the sixth day alongside man, but God subsequently created one of each land animal out of the ground of the Garden of Eden in front of Adam so that he could name it (Genesis 2:19). Adam was privileged to name the dinosaur kinds!

The word "dragon" appears 22 times in the Old Testament (King James Version of the Bible). The Psalmist writes: "Thou shalt tread upon the lion and adder: the young lion and the dragon shalt thou trample under feet" (Psalm 91:13). From the context it is clearly speaking about a real creature that would be impressive and intimidating to step on! Jeremiah states, "Nebuchadrezzar the king of Babylon hath devoured me, he hath crushed me, he hath made me an empty vessel, he hath swallowed me up like a dragon" (Jeremiah 51:34), which brings to mind the way many carnivorous reptiles crush and gulp their prey whole. Both dragons of the sea (Psalm 74:13) and field (Isaiah 43:20) are mentioned. Since the authorized version of the Bible was translated in 1611, the English word "dinosaur" doesn't appear in it. (The term wasn't invented for another 231 years.) But let's consider just a few biblical candidates for the great reptiles.

## Plesiosaur?

In Ezekiel 32:2 the prophet likens Pharaoh to a sea monster that invaded the Nile River and stirred up the mud. The Hebrew word "tannin" is from the root meaning "to extend." The language conjures up an image of a long-necked creature paddling up the river and stirring up mud from the Nile delta with its flippers. Such a creature is depicted on a seal (below) made by the ancient Egyptians who may have netted one just as Ezekiel describes in verse 3.

# Behemoth

Job, one of the oldest books in the Bible, tells the story of a tragedy in the life of the patriarch Job. Along the way, God points Job to two special creatures. The first, mentioned in Job 40:15, is usually translated "behemoth" in the English Bible.

Some commentators have suggested that behemoth was a hippo or elephant. But the verse makes clear that this herbivorous animal was "chief of the ways of God." Certainly the hippo and elephant (which had other Hebrew names) don't qualify as the biggest land animal, nor does their anatomy fit the clear language of Job 40:17, which tells how "he moves his tail like a cedar tree."

The cedar was the largest and strongest tree in the Middle East. The description brings to mind a dinosaur's huge tail being used as a club. Here we see an interesting and improbable convergence of information:

 The pygmy peoples in equatorial Africa tell stories of the Mokele-Mbembe that occupies their swamps and attacks opponents with its tail. [34]

 Modern paleontologists have theorized for some time that the mighty sauropod tails would have been useful as a weapon. It has even been suggested that diplodocids could have used their tails like a bullwhip, achieving supersonic cracks to intimidate enemies.[35]

 *The Aberdeen Bestiary*, a medieval volume written in the early 1500s and preserved in the library of Henry VIII, shows a dragon ensnarling an elephant and states: "Its strength lies not in its teeth but in its tail, and it kills with a blow rather than a bite."[36]

 Note also this fascinating biblical description of Satan: "And there appeared another wonder in heaven; and behold a great red dragon. . . . And his tail drew the third part of the stars of heaven, and did cast them to the earth" (Revelation 12:3–4). The tail is the offensive weapon of the dragon!

# Leviathan

Job 41 presents yet another incredible ancient creature: leviathan. While clearly one of the fiercest creatures that God made, it is difficult to establish exactly what leviathan was. The Bible describes a sharp-toothed, scaled creature whose habitat is the mire and deep waters.

Some have suggested the ferocious swimming Kronosaurus or a super crocodilian like Sarcosuchus as a candidate. Others have theorized that this vicious monster was a land-dweller that merely spent much of its time in the water. Perhaps leviathan was a dinosaur with armor or claws whose "sharp stones" were employed to destroy ancient weapons. Maybe we have yet to discover the remains of a leviathan.

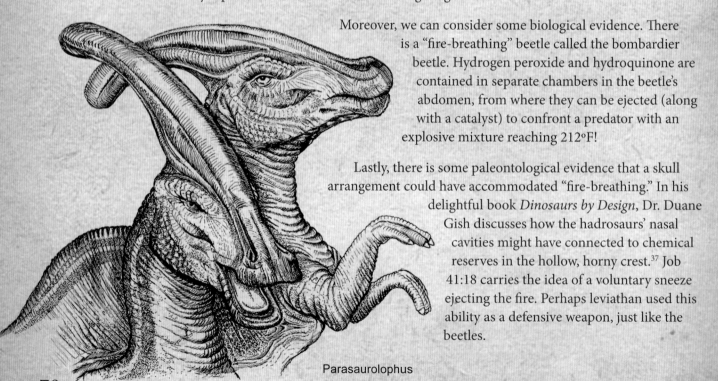

Sarcosuchus

But one thing is particularly fascinating: leviathans could breathe fire. The Bible leaves no room for hyperbole or a metaphoric interpretation. The Scripture says of leviathan, "Out of his mouth go burning lamps, and sparks of fire leap out. Out of his nostrils goeth smoke as out of a seething pot or caldron. His breath kindleth coals, and a flame goeth out of his mouth" (Job 41:19–21). There is also the matter of historical evidence. That is, multiple societies that were widely separated tell stories of fire-breathing dragons.

Moreover, we can consider some biological evidence. There is a "fire-breathing" beetle called the bombardier beetle. Hydrogen peroxide and hydroquinone are contained in separate chambers in the beetle's abdomen, from where they can be ejected (along with a catalyst) to confront a predator with an explosive mixture reaching 212°F!

Lastly, there is some paleontological evidence that a skull arrangement could have accommodated "fire-breathing." In his delightful book *Dinosaurs by Design*, Dr. Duane Gish discusses how the hadrosaurs' nasal cavities might have connected to chemical reserves in the hollow, horny crest.[37] Job 41:18 carries the idea of a voluntary sneeze ejecting the fire. Perhaps leviathan used this ability as a defensive weapon, just like the beetles.

Parasaurolophus

This fearsome fire-breathing creature is used by God to make the point in verse 10 that it is frightening to stand before the Creator. Indeed, the Bible describes God Himself as a consuming fire (Hebrews 12:29).

The leviathan is also mentioned in the Psalms: "So is this great and wide sea, wherein are things creeping innumerable, both small and great beasts. There go the ships: there is that leviathan, whom thou hast made to play therein" (Psalm 104:25–26). The association of ships and leviathan in this verse suggests that ancient mariners saw them. Perhaps a species of the fierce leviathan survives today, lurking deep in the ocean depths, a sea monster that still awaits discovery!

## BIBLE PUZZLER:

This chapter discussed some of the Old Testament verses mentioning the word "dragon." All dozen New Testament mentions of "dragon" come from a single book, and reference a single person. What is the book? Who is this person? Why do you think that person is likened to a dragon?

"Destruction of Leviathan," 1865 engraving by Gustave Dore

## The Fiery Flying Serpent

In the King James Version of Scripture we find Isaiah twice mentioning a fascinating reptilian flying creature. "The burden of the beasts of the south: into the land of trouble and anguish, from whence come the young and old lion, the viper and fiery flying serpent" (Isaiah 30:6). This verse distinguishes the fiery flying serpent from the viper. The prophet also states: "Rejoice not thou, whole Palestina, because the rod of him that smote thee is broken: for out of the serpent's root shall come forth a cockatrice, and his fruit shall be a fiery flying serpent" (Isaiah 14:29). Here the same creature is listed in a progression of animals, and is distinguished from the serpent and the cockatrice. What exactly is this ancient flying serpent referenced by the prophet Isaiah?

Creationists like Ken Ham of Answers in Genesis have suggested that this flying reptilian creature was a living pterosaur, still known in the region of Palestine at the time of Isaiah's prophecy.[38] Isaiah describes Egypt as the place of the fiery flying serpent (30:6), which matches classical authors' descriptions of pterosaur populations in Egypt and Arabia.

The Hebrew word used by Isaiah when describing this creature is *saraph*. The same Hebrew word is employed by the prophet to describe the heavenly beings that fly around God's throne (Isaiah 6) and comes from a root that means "to burn" or "to kindle." Might these flying attendants have appeared like the fiery flying serpents that Isaiah knew in his day?

It would be akin to John's recording of them in Revelation 4:6–8, where he likens these six-winged seraphim to specific animals. But unlike John, Isaiah did not see their faces in his vision; for they covered their heads with two wings and their legs with two wings, leaving only their hands (Isaiah 6:2) and trunks uncovered. Perhaps they looked to him like svelte, glowing, pterosaurs. (See the graphical comparison below.)

## Serpent on the Pole

The only other circumstance in which this Hebrew word saraph is used in Scripture is the famous event involving snakes in Numbers 21. The children of Israel had been forced to travel south toward the Gulf of Aqaba (into what is modern Saudi Arabia) because the nation of Edom had refused them passage. Lacking water and increasingly contemptuous of the heavenly manna provided, these murmuring Israelites faced God's judgment. "And the Lord sent fiery serpents *[saraphim nahashim]* among the people, and they bit the people; and much people of Israel died" (Numbers 21:6).

John Goertzen notes that the traditional interpretation of attacking venomous snakes seems problematic.[39] Firstly, the biblical account indicates that many of the Jews died (probably thousands). Obviously, God could miraculously do whatever He wished, but one has a hard time envisioning the people being pursued across the wilderness by slithering poisonous snakes. Common snakes should have easily been avoided once people were alerted to the danger.

Furthermore, the Bible says in Numbers 21:6 that God "sent" these venomous serpents and in verse 7 the Israelites requested that God "take away" the serpents. This language seems to imply highly mobile creatures that could come and go from that region.

Secondly, we note in verse 8: "And the Lord said unto Moses, Make thee a fiery serpent, and set it upon a pole: and it shall come to pass, that every one that is bitten, when he looketh upon it, shall live." In John 3:14-15 Jesus likens himself to that serpent placed on the pole. Yet it seems strange to employ the snake (a symbol of Satan from Genesis 3:1 to Revelation 20:2) as the parallel of Christ.

# Interpretation

It has been suggested by noted Bible scholars (like Matthew Henry and John Gill) that the creatures referenced here may be the flying serpents. This interpretation seems to fit the context quite well. These flying snakes, or pterosaurs, could have been sent to attack and overcome the Israelites from the air. The bronze flying serpent seems to be a more appropriate picture of the crucified Messiah than the cursed snake. Moreover, a pterosaur mounted on a pole with outstretched wings would have formed a cross.

The fiery serpent on a pole artifact was preserved in Israel for many subsequent generations and had become an idolatrous symbol by Hezekiah's reign (2 Kings 18:4). During that time, Sennacherib conquered much of Israel (2 Kings 18:13). It is interesting to note that a plate found with Sennacherib's booty at Calah depicts such a winged serpent on a pole that seems to match the Nehushtan or brazen saraph of Moses.

The description of the creatures as "fiery" brings to mind the cryptozoological reports from Papua New Guinea, which attribute to alleged living pterosaurs a brilliant bioluminescent capability. It also matches some of the dragon reports (see chapter 4) that ascribe brightness and glow to the flying dragons.

Plate from Sennacherib's booty

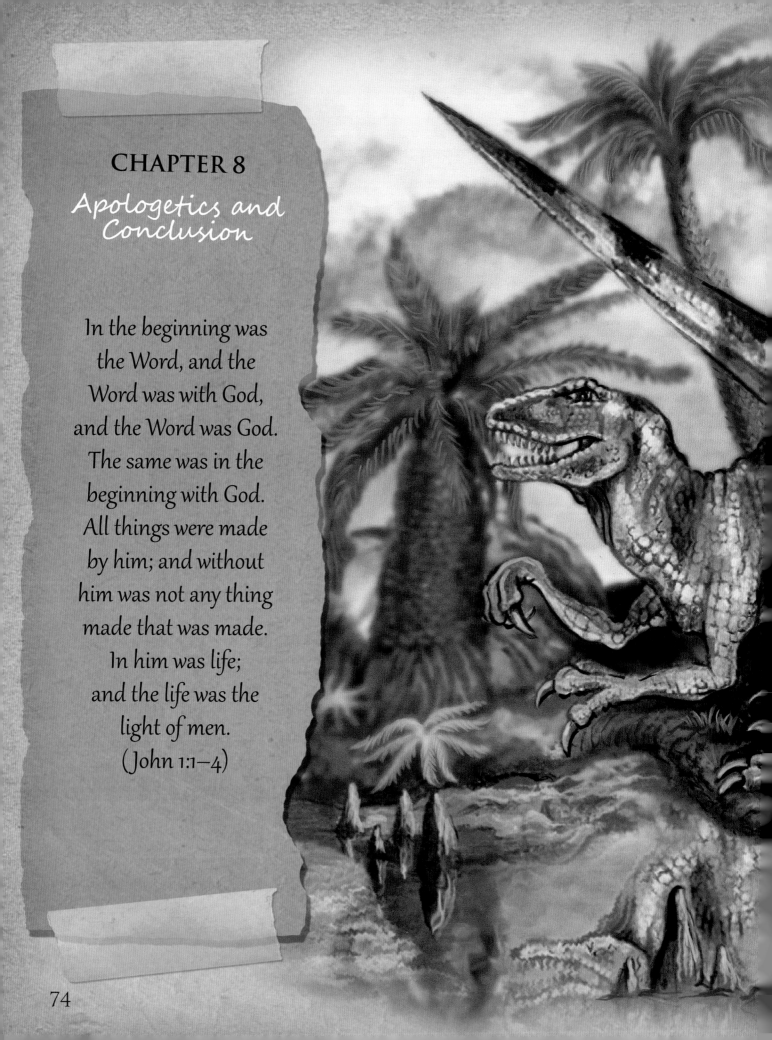

# CHAPTER 8
## Apologetics and Conclusion

In the beginning was the Word, and the Word was with God, and the Word was God. The same was in the beginning with God. All things were made by him; and without him was not any thing made that was made. In him was life; and the life was the light of men. (John 1:1–4)

Chapter 5 discusses the fascinating Ropen of Papua New Guinea and how it possesses a bioluminescent ability, like a glow worm and some deep-sea fish. Chapter 6 explains how well this evidence matches the biblical "fiery flying serpent" of the Old Testament. But Jesus appropriated the narrative concerning Israel and the fiery serpents as a type of His work: "And as Moses lifted up the serpent in the wilderness, even so must the Son of man be lifted up: That whosoever believeth in him should not perish, but have eternal life" (John 3:14–15).

The parallel is too obvious to miss. Just as the Hebrew people were bitten by the venom of the serpent (typifying Satan), so we are poisoned by sin. Unable to help ourselves, we are destined for sure death and separation from God. However, Jesus, like the brass serpent on the pole, was lifted up on the Cross and bore the punishment for our sins. The gospel (good news) is that we can look in faith to Him, just as the children of Israel in obedience looked up to the image on the pole. This believing look of faith will save us just as surely as it did them.

In Chapter 1 we noted that God shut the door on the wicked generation of Noah's day, effectively ending the opportunity for that civilization to repent of their disobedience and enter the place of refuge. But Jesus warned of a similar closing of the door at the end of this age. "But as the days of Noe were, so shall also the coming of the Son of man be. For as in the days that were before the flood they were eating and drinking, marrying and giving in marriage, until the day that Noe entered into the ark, And knew not until the flood came, and took them all away; so shall also the coming of the Son of man be" (Matthew 24:37–39).

The countdown has already begun on our generation. It is essential to be ready lest "When once the master of the house is risen up, and hath shut to the door, and ye begin to stand without, and to knock at the door, saying, Lord, Lord, open unto us; and he shall answer and say unto you, I know you not whence ye are" (Luke 13:25).

The information in this scrapbook is not designed merely to educate with fascinating facts and pictures regarding dinosaurs. Rather, the objective is to strengthen faith in God's Word and provide a defense for the literal, straightforward interpretation of Genesis. The five key points provided should confirm that our ancestors did indeed live alongside the great reptiles. This evidence forcefully and

clearly contradicts the evolutionary time scale and threatens the credibility of Darwinists who have stated unequivocally that men and dinosaurs never coexisted.

The anti-creationist Philip Kitcher admitted that solid evidence demonstrating the coexistence of dinosaurs and man would "shake the foundations of evolutionary theory."[41] I am hopeful that we will soon discover a living dinosaur, plesiosaur, or pterosaur to demonstrate contemporary co-existence beyond any doubt.

Dinosaurs are indeed awe-inspiring creatures that fascinate old and young alike. The great reptiles occupy an important place in the divine message of creation. After describing the dreadful leviathan, the Lord said, "None is so fierce that dare stir him up: who then is able to stand before me?" (Job 41:10). This tells us that God's purpose in making fearsome creatures like behemoth and leviathan is to show His greatness and power. In this sense, dinosaurs truly are living evidence of a powerful Creator!

Mamenchisaurus

Thescelosaurus

## Dino Dave's Challenge

For the Bible-believing Christian, the authoritative Old Testament record settles the matter of dinosaurs co-existing with man. But it is gratifying to find extensive fossil, historical, artistic, and cryptozoology evidence as well. Merely believing that dinosaurs were created as Genesis claims, however, falls short of the core message of God's Word.

One must go beyond the account of creation to find the message of God's redemption of a world that fell into sin and judgment.

If you have not yet placed your faith in Jesus Christ as your Savior, I would challenge you to read the Scripture for yourself and prayerfully consider the Plan of Salvation given to the right. My challenge for Christians is to employ dinosaurs as God did in the Book of Job.

Let us use contemporary society's natural attraction to these imposing reptiles to point friends and relatives to our magnificent, loving, and powerful Creator!

The day is coming when God will restore the wonderful environment of the early Earth, establishing a marvelous kingdom to be enjoyed by all whose sins have been forgiven (Isaiah 65:17-25). Fearsome animals will once again peacefully cohabitate with man, including any living dinosaurian creatures.

# God's Plan of Salvation

1. You are a sinner. "For all have sinned, and come short of the glory of God" (Romans 3:23).

2. The penalty for sin is eternal death, separation from God. "For the wages of sin is death; but the gift of God is eternal life through Jesus Christ our Lord" (Romans 6:23).

3. Jesus died as a substitute, paying your penalty. "But God commendeth his love toward us, in that, while we were yet sinners, Christ died for us" (Romans 5:8).

4. If you repent and call upon Christ to save you, He promises you eternal life as a free gift. "For whosoever shall call upon the name of the Lord shall be saved" (Romans 10:13).

Won't you turn from your sin today and acknowledge your need for a Savior? Ask God to forgive you and grant you salvation.

We would be delighted to hear from you if you have made a decision to accept Jesus Christ as your Savior or if you have any questions about creation, Christianity, or dinosaurs. Visit us at www.GenesisPark.com and fill out the contact form.

# ENDNOTES

1. Sean Carroll, *Endless Forms Most Beautiful* (New York: W.W. Norton & Company, Inc., 2005), p. 295.

2. Anonymous, "Geoguide: Age of Dinosaurs," *National Geographic* 183 (January, 1993): p. 142.

3. Michael Ruse and Joseph Travis, *Evolution: The First Four Billion Years* (Cambridge, MA: Harvard University Press, 2009), p. 518.

4. Michael Novacek, "Fossils of the Flaming Cliffs," *Scientific American* 271 (December, 1994): p. 60–69.

5. Richard Milner, *The Encyclopedia of Evolution: Humanity's Search for Its Origins* (New York: Facts on File, Inc., 1990), p. 330.

6. See Michael Cremo, and Richard Thompson, *Forbidden Archaeology: The Hidden History of the Human Race* (Los Angeles, CA: Bhaktivedanta Institute, 1996).

7. Glen J. Kuban, "The Paluxy Dinosaur/'Man Track' Controversy," http://paleo.cc/paluxy. htm, accessed 4/27/2012.

8. Brian Handwerk, "Easter Surprise: World's Oldest Rabbit Bones Found," *National Geographic News*, March 2008, http://news.nationalgeographic.com/ news/2008/03/080321-rabbit-bones.html, accessed 5/11/2012.

9. Don Batten, "Living Fossils: A Powerful Argument for Creation," *Creation* 33 (March, 2011): p. 20.

10. Kyle L. Davies, "Duckbill Dinosaurs (*Hadrosauridae*, Ornithisichia) from the North Slope of Alaska," *Journal of Paleontology* 61 (January, 1987): p. 198–200.

11. See Buddy Davis, John Whitmore, and Mike Liston, *The Great Alaskan Dinosaur Adventure* (Green Forest, AR: Master Books, 1999).

12. Wilson Knox, "Dragon," *The World Book Encyclopedia* 5 (Chicago, IL: World Book Inc., 1973), p. 265.

13. Carl Sagan, *The Dragons of Eden* (New York: Random House, 1977), p. 149.

14. Marco Polo, *The Travels of Marco Polo*, (New York: Signet Classics, 1961), p. 158–159.

15. Doug Zhiming, *Dinosaurs From China* (Beijing: China Ocean Press, 1988), p. 9.

16. Ulysses Aldrovandus, *The Natural History of Serpents and Dragons* (Bologna: Mark Antony Bernia, 1640), p.402.

17. Herodotus, *Historiae*, trans. Henry Clay (London: Henry G. Bohn, 1850), p. 75–76.

18. Marie Trevelyan, *Folk-Lore and Folk Stories of Wales* (Yorkshire: EP Publishing Ltd., 1973), p. 168.

19. Athanasius Kircher, *Mundus Subterraneus*, 1664, trans. by Peter Hogarth in *Dragons* (New York: The Viking Press, 1979), p. 179–180.

20. Karl Shuker, *Dragons: A Natural History* (New York: Simon & Schuster, 1995), p. 8.

21. Stephen Czerkas, "New Look for Sauropod Dinosaurs," *Geology* 20 (December, 1992): p. 1,068.

22. Bernard Heuvelmans, *Les Derniers Dragons d'Afrique* (Paris: Plon, 1978), p. 336–337.

23. Paul S. Taylor, *The Great Dinosaur Mystery and the Bible* (Colorado Springs, CO: Chariot Victor Publishing, 1989), p. 38.

24. Vance Nelson, *Dire Dragons* (Alberta: Untold Secrets of Planet Earth Publishing Company, 2011), p. 100.

25. Peter Wellnhofer, *The Illustrated Encyclopedia of Pterosaurs* (New York: Crescent Books, 1991), p. 20.

26. http://s8int.com/dinolit35. html, accessed 9/1/2012.

27. Lucien Blancou, "Notes Sur les Mammifères de l'Equateur Africain Français: Un Rhinocéros de Fôret?" *Mammalia 18*, trans. Bernard Heuvelmans (December 1954): p. 358–363.

28. Roy Mackal, *A Living Dinosaur* (Leiden: E.J. Brill, 1987), p. 247.

29. Anonymous, "Living Dinosaurs," *Science–80* 1 (November 1980): p. 6–7

30. Karl Shuker, *Dragons: A Natural History* (New York: Simon & Schuster, 1995), p. 38.

31. See Pau LeBlond, and Edward Bousfield, *Cadborosaurus: Survivor from the Deep* (Victoria: Horsdal and Schubart, 1995).

32. Joseph W. Zarzynski, *Champ: Beyond the Legend* (Port Henry: Bannister Publications, 1984), p.82.

33. Arlene Gaal, *In Search of Ogopogo* (Surrey: Hancock House Publishers Ltd., 2001), p. 13.

34. For more information, see Dave Woetzel, "Behemoth or Bust: An Expedition into Cameroon Investigating Reports of a Sauropod Dinosaur," *Creation Journal* 15 (August 2001): p. 62–68.

35. Nathan P. Myhrvold and Philip J. Currie, "Supersonic Sauropods? Tail Dynamics in the Diplodocids," *Paleobiology* 23 (December 1997): p. 393–409.

36. Archived at Aberdeen University by Michael Arnott, original work circa 1200, http://www.abdn.ac.uk/bestiary/translat/65v.hti, accessed 4/27/12.

37. Duane Gish, *Dinosaurs by Design* (Green Forest, AR: Master Books, 1992), p.82.

38. Ken Ham, *The Great Dinosaur Mystery Solved!* (Green Forest, AR: Master Books, 1999), p. 45.

39. John Goertzen, "The Bible and Pterosaurs: Archaeological and Linguistic Studies of Jurassic Animals that Lived Recently," 1998, http://www.rae.org/pteroets.html, accessed 10/4/2011.

40. Matthew Henry, *A Commentary on the Whole Bible* (Peabody, MA: Hendrickson Publishers, Inc., 1992), p. 520.

41. Philip Kitcher, *Abusing Science* (Cambridge, MA: MIT Press, 1998), p. 121.

Protoceratops

## Author Profile

"Dino Dave" Woetzel was privileged to grow up in a Christian home and, as a child, accepted Christ as his personal Savior. He was fascinated with dinosaurs at an early age and grew to love science. Dave graduated from Bob Jones University in 1987 with a bachelor of science degree. He currently resides with his wife, Gloria, and two children in Concord, New Hampshire, where he is the president of CCR Data Systems, a technology firm. Dave has had numerous opportunities to speak on the topic of science and the Bible around the world. In 1999, Dave started the Genesis Park website which showcases evidence that men and dinosaurs coexisted, much of which is now included in this book. He has also spearheaded some fascinating expeditions that have earned him the nickname "Dino Dave." These include a trip into the unexplored African rainforest of Cameroon; travel to a remote volcanic island in Papua New Guinea; an expedition up the Amazon through the Madidi River in Bolivia; an investigation into the swamps of Lake Bangweulu, Zambia; research at Scotland's Loch Ness; pursuit of swimming monsters in Lake Champlain and Lake Okanagan in North America; and research on Lake Nahuel Haupi in South America. One of his favorite Bible verses is:

*"Hast thou not known? hast thou not heard, that the everlasting God, the Lord, the Creator of the ends of the earth, fainteth not, neither is weary? there is no searching of his understanding"* (Isaiah 40:28).

## Illustrator Profile

Richard D. Dobbs Jr. was born in Atlanta, Georgia, and also grew up with Christian parents. He was a dinosaur fan for as long as he can remember and began drawing pictures of the great reptiles at an early age. Richard discovered he had gifts in art and music and desired to spend his life devoting these gifts to God's glory. While still a young man, Richard experienced God's love and grace and, at the age of 13, was baptized to publicly confess his devotion to Christ. After high school, Richard enlisted in the U.S. Marine Corps and was assigned to Camp Pendleton where he played in the band. In 1990 he participated in Desert Storm as an M-60 Gunner, providing security detail. In 1991 he showed his personal art portfolio to the Camp Pendleton Art Department and was accepted into their graphics team despite his lack of formal training. After leaving the Marines, Richard earned an associate's degree in commercial art from Johnston Community College in Smithfield, North Carolina. Richard works as a freelance artist and graphic illustrator. He enjoys fine art projects like portraits, paintings, murals, and book illustrations. Richard lives near Raleigh, North Carolina, with his wife, Carrie, and three daughters. His favorite Scripture passage is:

*"I am crucified with Christ: nevertheless I live; yet not I, but Christ liveth in me: and the life which I now live in the flesh I live by the faith of the Son of God, who loved me, and gave himself for me"* (Galatians 2:20).

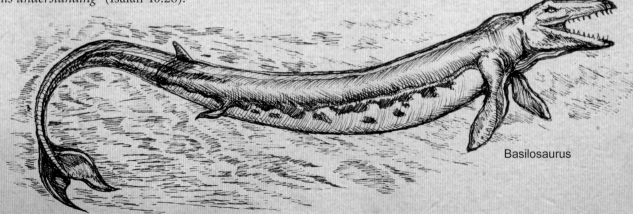

Basilosaurus

# CRYPTOZOOLOGY EXPEDITION:

Visit www.GenesisPark.com to learn about more cryptid locations around the world and get news on upcoming expeditions. Perhaps one of these places where dinosaurian creatures have reportedly been sighted is near where you live. Wouldn't it be exciting to take a trip and do some research? Bring a pair of binoculars and a good camera!

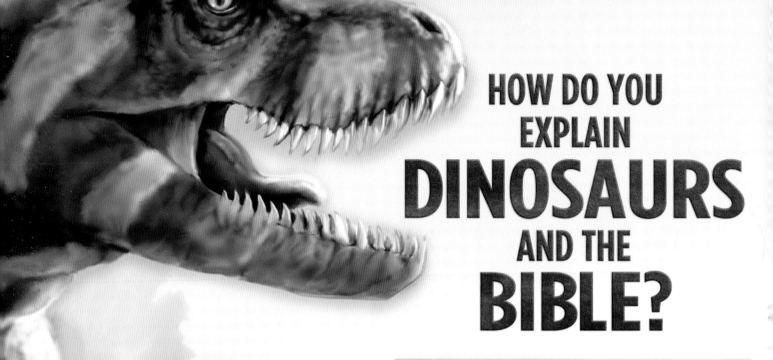

# HOW DO YOU EXPLAIN DINOSAURS AND THE BIBLE?

**ebook**

for the ipad only

Loaded with video, audio pronunciations, 3D imagery, educational pop outs, and more!

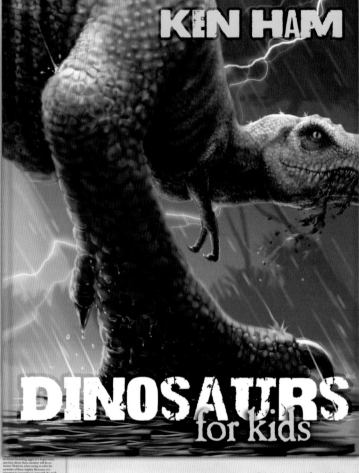

KEN HAM

**DINOSAURS** for kids

Master Books®
A Division of New Leaf Publishing Group
www.masterbooks.net

**Available in bookstores nationwide or call 1.800.999.3777 to order your copies.**

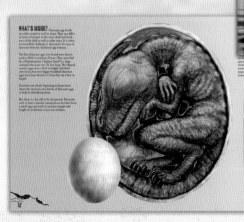

Information-packed and powerfully presented, *Dinosaurs for Kids* (ages 7 to 12) is the one book on dinosaurs every family should own. Author Ken Ham, one of the most in-demand Christian speakers in North America, takes dinosaur lovers on an exciting, revealing, and simply amazing journey through time.

8.5 x 11 • 64 pages • Casebound • Full Color Interior
ISBN: 978-0-89051-555-6 • $14.99 u.s.